I0819935

"*A Hundred Years of Childhood* is a unique anthology of Russian children's literature both in its temporal scope and in its selection of poetic and prose texts. High-quality translation considers all the nuances of the realities the English-speaking reader will encounter as they become familiar with these texts. The editors of the collection were able to show what tasks—genre, aesthetic, and social—the literature set for itself throughout the centuries. The anthology is a priceless resource for researchers—historians, cultural studies scholars, and literary scholars—but it is equally interesting to a wide circle of readers, for whom the translation serves as a bridge to understanding another culture."

Marina Balina, Isaac Funk Professor Emerita of Russian Studies, Illinois Wesleyan University

"Despite its academic appeal, this anthology of the last 100 years of Russian children's literature has a very good chance of becoming a book that you will read to your children and grandchildren before bedtime, and that they will secretly read after you put them to bed. There are three reasons for this. It is filled with true gems handpicked by editors from the rich legacy of Soviet children's literature. It is enhanced by the best examples of post-Soviet writings for children. It is conveyed into English by truly congenial translations. All in all, these texts will make you and your kids laugh and think about the most interesting and serious things in the world—from games and toys to revolutions, nature, family, school, friends, history and the future. Teaching classes with this book will be a sheer pleasure for students and professors alike. I envy them already."

Mark Lipovetsky, Professor and Chair, Department of Slavic Languages, Columbia University

"Across the one-hundred-year period that began with the Bolshevik Revolution of 1917, children's literature written in Russian has encapsulated the hopes and aspirations of a far-flung society caught in a maelstrom of social and political change. This thoughtfully curated treasury of writings in translation by thirty-six notable authors for young people immerses readers in a deeply serious and often exhilarating literary tradition that, in all its many moods and permutations, has continually homed in on the core concerns that fuel children's imaginations."

Leonard S. Marcus, Children's book historian and critic

"*A Hundred Years of Childhood: An Anthology of Russian Writing for Children, 1917–2017* is an insightfully framed collection of charming stories and poems from the Russian-speaking world that bring moments from one hundred tumultuous years of history into sharp focus through the lens of children's literature. The array of poems and stories selected for the collection speak powerfully for themselves through varied, charming, and inspired new translations that grant access to these stories for contemporary English-speaking audiences. At the same time, the carefully curated anthology richly situates authors and illustrators within their own complex contexts and also includes imagery from original book publications in a variety of styles. This anthology will appeal to popular audiences of all ages and will prove a useful tool for teaching Russian-language children's literature and culture in English-speaking contexts."

Sara Pankenier Weld, Professor, Department of Germanic and Slavic Studies, University of California, Santa Barbara

"Thanks to this new book, one hundred years of Russian children's literature comes alive in sparkling English translation. Olga Bukhina, Kelly Herold and Andrea Lanoux contextualize Soviet and post-Soviet texts with helpful and intelligent introductions. Beloved classics and exciting new voices in Russian children's literature can all be found here—and enjoyed by parents, children, teachers and students."

Megan Swift, Professor of Russian Studies, University of Victoria

A HUNDRED YEARS OF CHILDHOOD

An Anthology of Russian Writing for Children, 1917-2017

A HUNDRED YEARS OF CHILDHOOD

An Anthology of Russian Writing for Children, 1917-2017

Edited by Olga Bukhina,
Kelly Herold,
and Andrea Lanoux

CHERRY ORCHARD BOOKS
2026

Library of Congress Cataloging-in-Publication Data

Names: Bukhina, Ol'ga editor | Herold, Kelly, 1967- editor | Lanoux, Andrea editor
Title: A hundred years of childhood : an anthology of Russian writing for children, 1917-2017 / edited by Olga Bukhina, Kelly Herold, and Andrea Lanoux.
Description: Boston : Cherry Orchard Books, 2026. | Includes bibliographical references. | Contents: v. 1. -- v. 2.
Identifiers: LCCN 2025046613 (print) | LCCN 2025046614 (ebook) | ISBN 9798887198590 hardback | ISBN 9798887198606 adobe pdf | ISBN 9798887198613 epub
Subjects: LCSH: Children's poetry, Russian--Translations into English | Children's poetry, Russian--Translations into English | Russian poetry--20th century--Translations into English | Russian fiction--20th century--Translations into English | LCGFT: Poetry | Short stories | Excerpts | Fiction
Classification: LCC PG3213 .H86 2026 (print) | LCC PG3213 (ebook) LC record available at https://lccn.loc.gov/2025046613 LC ebook record available at https://lccn.loc.gov/202504661

Copyright © Academic Studies Press, 2026, English translation, collection

ISBN 9798887198590 (hardback)
ISBN 9798887198606 (Adobe PDF)
ISBN 9798887198613 (ePub)

Book design by PHi Business Solutions
Cover design by Ivan Grave. Cover illustration by Anna Desnitskaya

Published by Cherry Orchard Books, an imprint of Academic Studies Press
1007 Chestnut St.
Newton, MA 02464, USA
press@academicstudiespress.com
www.academicstudiespress.com

Contents

Acknowledgments

This collection is largely the work of other people: dozens of texts written by three dozen writers, translated into English by a score of literary translators. We are grateful to the authors whose extraordinary creativity graces this volume, and to the specialists whose sensitivity and skill with language make these texts accessible across linguistic, cultural, and historical divides.

Children's literature conveys the aspirations and dreams of a given culture. These works embody the unique hopes of those who endeavored to create the world's first equal society. We are indebted to the generations of children who inspired these works, to the adults who read to them, and to the readers today who continue to bring them to life.

We are likewise thankful to the individuals who brought this anthology to fruition. Our sincere gratitude goes to Mark Lipovetsky, who inspired this volume in its early stages; to Christina Dunbar and Christian P. Winting from Columbia University Press, who helped shape its first iteration; and to Igor Nemirovsky and Daniel Frese of Academic Studies Press, who rescued the project after the devastating impact of Russia's full-scale invasion of Ukraine became clear. Many thanks to Stuart Allen and Ilya Nikolaev for their eagle-eyed editing and thoughtful comments. Finally, we deeply appreciate Grinnell and Connecticut Colleges for their continued support, including for this volume.

This anthology would not have come into being without the heirs and agents of the authors and artists whose beautiful work fills these pages. Thank you for giving these texts a second life. And to our families, near and far, thank you for your patience, encouragement, and love.

List of Illustrations

Foreword

Surely one of the things that connects us across even the most inflexible cultural barriers is the recognition that the arts can speak to and for childhood. Perhaps this comes about as the artist expresses an emotion, or memory, or insight that is completely recognizable to the child receiving the art. Perhaps it comes about when the artist and the child meet over some comic or poignant moment, where the emotion or experience is mutually recognized, despite even a huge age difference, as the adult memory and the child experience meet. Or perhaps it occurs when the artist's work is able to express empathy over the vulnerability of the child life, where so much is decided for her and power or choice seems outside the child's reach.

It may be that the power of this recognition transcends all the barriers that differing cultures build, so that the child and the artist can meet, can recognize each other's experience, and can come very, very close to true and deep empathy and understanding.

Thus the pleasures of an anthology of Russian writing for children at a time when such understanding across cultures seems so unlikely. Risking a cliché from a Disneyland attraction, "There's so much that we share"—or, there's so much that we recognize and affirm together about the experience of childhood.

A quatrain from Alexander Vvedensky's "Lullaby" inventively evokes a universal experience through its rhythms and repeating sounds:

> Sleep, it walks up to your bed,
> And it yawns and whispers still:
> Trees and Bushes have retired,
> Fall asleep, my tired Child.

Agnia Barto's "The House That Moved" amplifies the desperate fear of loss and abandonment that a child might have when Mitya returns home from camp to find that his house is gone:

> I came home from the Black Sea.
> Home is where I need to be!
> That big building shouldn't hide—
> I have left my mom inside!

Boris Zakhoder's "Cooks" affirms a moment of recognition when a young child understands his mother's skills:

> But sometimes Mama is not home,
> And we have to make [dinner] all on our own,
> And then
> (who knows why, I'm just a beginner!)
> It's very
> Tricky
> Making
> Dinner!

Reading an anthology such as this emphasizes the commonalities of childhood, no matter the culture. The staccato repetitions of Barto's "Bedtime" powerfully express the longing for connection between a child and a parent:

> Look, the lights are being lit
> Round the block.
> Almost bedtime.
> Let's just sit,
> Sit and talk.
> All day long,
> I never can
> Talk to you.
> All you have is work to do,
> Work to do . . .
> Let's just sit,
> Sit and talk.

How powerfully this chimes with Masha Rupasova's "I Am News," which modernizes the situation but not the sentiment:

> Where is Mommy? Far away!
> She's been facebooking all day . . .
> Mom? Hello? You've got to hear:
> I am happening right here!

In the stressed and fraught world in which we live, it is healthy to perceive the commonalities of childhood experiences. And it is healthy too to see the variety that cultures can bring to the expression of these commonalities. Thus, for example, Daniil Kharms's Mr. Golden Samovar's chastising voice against laziness when Boris comes down late, yawning and asking for a cup of tea:

> Everybody
> Everybody,
> Tipped the samovar
> Tip tip tip.
> But the only thing they got
> Was
> A tiny
> Drip drip drip.

Or Eduard Uspensky's child-character Uncle Fedya, who runs away from home to protect his cat, finds a dog and buried treasure, and who lives in a small village and uses his wealth to buy a tractor that runs on potatoes—a world of entire self-sufficiency, until Uncle Fedya gets ill.

And in an anthology that begins in the Soviet era and concludes in post-Soviet times, we see a literature that morphs with the questions of its time. It is certainly true that children's literature is about the experience of the child, but the questions that same literature poses, and the answers those questions may generate, shift with the changing perspectives of what children's literature is meant to be and do from the point of view of the generating culture. In the West, that might mean shifts from prescription to urge the child reader to adhere to specific cultural norms, to description about how those norms are subverted in places like the land of the Wild Things. In Soviet and contemporary Russian literature, that means a focus on rapid social change—and a reevaluation of children's literature that was once seen as unifying, and may now be perceived as hegemonic.

And perhaps, in both cultures, the word *subversive* might itself be more than a little appropriate when referencing children's books. After all, Grigory Oster's *Horrible Advice: A Book for Disobedient Children and Their Caregivers* and Dr. Seuss's *The Cat in the Hat* both suggest a world where children—like adults—have their own interior being that cannot and should not be violated, even by those loving adults who support them. And what could be more subversive than arguing for the sanctity of a private interior life?

Perhaps that is the most important commonality in children's books.

—Gary D. Schmidt
Alto, MI
April 2025

INTRODUCTION

The Enduring Power of Children's Literature in Times of Social Change

Children's literature reveals much about the society in which it emerged, since one of its key functions is to transmit the culture of that society to future citizens. While all cultural artifacts disclose features of the society that produced them, the knowledge gap between adult authors and the child readers they write for makes children's literature a unique site of cultural production—a field of education, acculturation, and engagement across generations all at the same time. In the case of Russian children's literature from the early twentieth century to the beginning of the twenty-first, the tumultuous history of Soviet communism and its collapse in 1991 makes the process of cultural transmission especially complicated, due to rifts in the ideological and aesthetic qualities of texts produced in the imperial Russian, Soviet, and post-Soviet eras. Texts written in Russian for children over the long twentieth century are among the most fascinating and potent works in the Russian language, laying bare the dreams of early Soviet activists to educate a new generation of children deeply committed to the common good, as well as the dashed hopes of their successors in the 1990s who bitterly witnessed the failure of the world's first social justice project on a mass scale. Soviet children's literature is still enjoyed by millions of readers today, and its legacy remains one that twenty-first-century writers must reckon with in their own works for young readers.

As we bring this collection to print, Russia's ongoing war in Ukraine has made it all too clear that history never stops: the violence and repression of authoritarian rule that defined the Soviet period has resurfaced in full view, this time with the aim of subjugating a people that has developed different ideas about its political future through the process of strengthening its own civil society. The war has driven a piercing wedge between identity categories that were previously overlapping and opaque in Soviet times, such as language, ethnicity, and citizenship. Like all works written in Russian, texts for children are now being reread by scholars and lay readers with an eye to the hegemonic sensibilities running through them: the "friendship of peoples" ethos that dominates so much of Soviet children's literature is now seen in a new and nefarious light, casting children as key actors in a colonizing project that employs literacy, language, and assimilation policies to create a "new" people. Put differently, the Russo-Ukrainian War has exposed national identities and their embodiment in language categories that were previously masked over with broader political aims, ones that continue to have a direct impact on the lived experiences of children.

Today, the use of the word "Russian" to designate millions of people who may speak Russian, but who are not ethnic Russians or citizens of the Russian Federation, is often perceived as an act of violence in itself—one employed repeatedly by the Putin administration to justify its invasion of a sovereign state. So as to not repeat this gesture, we want to clarify our use of the term Russian in the title of this book. The focus of this anthology is literature for children *written in Russian* and published between 1917 and 2017. Some of the authors featured in this volume are ethnic Russians; others are Armenian, Georgian, Jewish, Ukrainian, or other ethnicities encompassed by the Soviet Empire. As a result, this anthology documents the extraordinary diversity of backgrounds of those who strove to advance children's literature and culture throughout the Soviet and post-Soviet periods, while at the same time illustrating the overall impact of this body of work in obscuring this diversity and making it invisible under the banner of "Russian."

It is all too evident from the conflicts unfolding in Ukraine, Russia, and elsewhere that political upheaval deeply impacts children's education, upbringing, and daily life. As this volume demonstrates, societal crisis and rapid social change are vividly reflected in the creation of cultural materials for children. The hundred-year period from 1917 to 2017 was a remarkably volatile and brutal one: the Bolshevik Revolution of 1917 and subsequent civil war, state-sponsored famine in Ukraine known as the Holodomor (1932–1933), Stalin's purges, World War II, and the fall of the Soviet state all brought radical changes to children's lives. We can now see these changes reflected on the pages of stories and books whose characters, plots, and systems of values have evolved over time. One overarching theme of Soviet-era children's books is their presentation of childhood as a joyous and magical time—a wondrous stage in life in which friends, family, and "the collective" bring happiness and meaning that is greater than individual concerns. The consistent refrain of the magical childhood, and the increasing sense that childhood became happier on the page as it became sadder in real life during the Stalin era and beyond, allow us to treat these works as a coherent literary tradition, one built on magic and melancholy, on childhood joy and tragedy.

Among the texts in this anthology are some of the most renowned and resonant works for children written in the Russian language, many of which appear here in English translation for the first time. This volume consists largely of literature for younger children, which in the Russophone tradition is dominated by the genres of the picture book, poetry, fairy tale, nature writing, stories about animals, and short prose. For readers who grew up in the Soviet Union, the Russian Federation, or another former Soviet state, most of these texts are well known. The extraordinary variety of children's texts produced in the USSR follows a clear arc of development, from the avant-garde writing of the 1920s to the heroism and patriotic fervor of the Stalin era; during Khrushchev's Thaw and beyond, texts tended to have a more modest scope, focusing on children's everyday life at school and at home. Many contemporary readers encountering these works for the first time express surprise at the high quality of the writing and illustrations, given the longstanding stereotype of Soviet literature as purely ideological with the aim of indoctrination.

Children's literature published after 1991 tends to be lesser known even among native speakers of Russian, when compared with the more robust Soviet children's canon. Only a handful of post-Soviet works for young readers have been published in English translation before now. The texts in Part 4, "New Russia, New Stories," are among the most acclaimed works published after 1989, when the fall of the Berlin Wall and rise of independent states in Eastern Europe, the Caucuses, and Central Asia led to rapid societal change and the eventual fall of the Soviet state. Despite their novelty and orientation toward a new turn in post-Soviet society, these works nevertheless reflect their Soviet heritage, melding this worldview with new ideas and genres. Globalizing forces are deeply felt in new literature for children published after 1991, marking the beginning of a new literary direction whose evolution has been stymied by an ongoing conservative backlash and by the designation of outside influences as nefarious "foreign agents." As this anthology goes to print, this most recent chapter in the development of Russian-language children's literature is still being written, sometimes against resurgent repression and censorship.

In selecting texts for this anthology, we invited over a dozen of the leading translators working in Russian and English today to participate, in order to ensure the preservation of a multitude of unique voices that are so strikingly felt in the original Russian texts. Translators assisted in the textual selection process, suggesting works that they especially admired, recalled vividly from their own childhoods, or wished to translate for personal reasons. Some members of our translation team speak Russian as their native language; others are native speakers of English who have been working in Russian for many years. Each translator has their own literary preferences, style, and philosophy of translation. Many of the authors represented in this volume pose particular challenges in bringing their work into in English: some are masters of the absurd (such as Daniil Kharms, Alexander Vvedensky, Nikolai Zabolotsky, Boris Zakhoder, Genrikh Sapgir, Oleg Grigoriev, and Irina Pivovarova), who found adherents and continuers of this mode of composition in later decades (among them Grigory Oster, Sergei Sedov, Mikhail Esenovsky, and Artur Givargizov). Wordplay, humor, and inventive language are central features of children's literature the world over, making the translation of these texts a creative act. We are proud to feature in this volume specialists whose solutions to translation problems never cease to awe with their creativity, and whose commitment to bringing both the sense and spirit of the original into English has been spectacularly fruitful.

In our 2022 book *Growing Out of Communism: Russian Literature for Children and Teens, 1917–2017*, we examine the evolution of a Soviet vision of childhood and the dramatic backlash to that vision following the fall of the Soviet state.[1] Although we will not repeat the arguments of that work here, we came to the conclusion while writing it that the Soviet canon of children's literature and works for children published after 1991 deserve to be known internationally, given their importance for understanding the effects of political crisis, the collapse of states, and globalization on children throughout the globe. The present anthology can be read as a companion to *Growing Out of Communism*, making the texts discussed in that study readily available and accessible in English. This anthology may also be read as a stand-alone book, giving children and adult readers access to these extraordinary works for their own sake, and the opportunity to develop their own interpretations, insights, and conclusions about the Soviet era and its aftermath.

Predictably, some of the important and influential writing from the Soviet period has not withstood the test of time. In selecting texts for this anthology, we decided to privilege those that continue to resonate with readers today. This decision resulted in the omission of many works that may have been widely read in their time, but have since been forgotten—stories about Lenin as a young boy, biographies of revolutionary heroes, epic poems featuring martyrs of the Great Patriotic War. While such texts are important documents that convey the mandates and sense of the times, we wished to showcase writing that transcends

---

1 Andrea Lanoux, Kelly Herold, and Olga Bukhina, *Growing Out of Communism: Russian Literature for Children and Teens, 1991–2017* (Paderborn: Brill-Schöningh, 2022).

its own era. Of course, textual selection always reflects the tastes and sensibilities of the editors: in our case, only one of us (Bukhina) grew up reading these texts; the other two (Herold and Lanoux) came to this material as American scholars of Russian literature. That said, all of us are committed to foregrounding influential children's fiction in order to illustrate the development of this body of work as a connected conversation.

Texts from the early Soviet period are most often the product of the enormous, state-run apparatus that commissioned, published, and disseminated them. Encompassing a wide array of institutions (publishing houses, distribution networks, children's libraries, school curricula, and the Soviet Writers Union), these institutions worked in a coordinated way to offer a particular, agreed upon set of values in order to educate children with the same ideological leanings in a consistent manner. What strikes us about early Soviet writers is their consciousness of, and open commitment to, their didacticism. Many of these writers were sincere adherents of the Soviet vision, which required that children receive a strong moral education with a focus on collectivism, compassion for the downtrodden, and a belief in the common good. The line between education and didacticism disappears in many of these works, making "texts that teach" a central part of the Soviet canon.

Poetry became a favorite medium of the early Soviets for channeling the creative energy of the revolution to children, in part because rhymed texts are foundational to oral traditions of children's culture before literacy, namely, to nursery rhymes and songs. Masterworks such as Kornei Chukovsky's "Telephone," "Roach the Terrible," and "Gottascrub," Samuil Marshak's "Baggage" and "Ice Cream," Vladimir Mayakovsky's "What Is Good and What Is Bad," and Alexander Vvedensky's "Who?" demonstrate the remarkable linguistic virtuosity evident in children's texts from the decade following the Bolshevik Revolution, as well as the messages embedded within them: children's ability to speak truth to power, the importance of good hygiene, and the excesses of capitalist greed. Given children's predisposition to language acquisition and their natural interest in rhymes and patterned speech, these works captured the imaginations of the youngest members of Soviet society, and quickly became beloved classics that are still read, recited, and enjoyed by Russian-speaking children and families today.

As the events of the Bolshevik Revolution began to recede into the past, the boundary between the Soviet and imperial periods became an exaggeratedly hard line that masked the deep ties between the tsarist past and communist present. Despite their desire to "throw Pushkin, Dostoevsky, Tolstoy," and other nineteenth-century writers "overboard the Ship of Modernity," as the Russian Futurists strove to do in their 1917 manifesto "A Slap in the Face of Public Taste," children's writers working in the first decades of Soviet power were deeply connected to their prerevolutionary predecessors, both within and outside Russia. Two of the most influential figures in the new Soviet children's literature, Kornei Chukovsky and Samuil Marshak, were Anglophiles whose works bear the influence of Lewis Carroll, Edward Lear, Mother Goose, and the British tradition of humor generally, which they rendered beautifully in Russian rhyme and meter. The absurdist tendencies of Daniil Kharms and Alexander Vvedensky, who belonged to the avant-garde Union of Real Art (OBERIU) based in Leningrad, echoed the Dadaist movement in Zürich—both of which were literary responses to rapid societal upheaval and the senseless violence of World War I. The influence of children's works in the Russian tradition, such as Pushkin's fairy tales, Petr Yershov's *The Little Humpbacked Horse*, and Antony Pogorelsky's *The Black Hen*, was also reflected in this growing body of work, despite many writers' categorical disavowal of the prerevolutionary past. Chukovsky's famous poem *Mukha-Tsokotukha* (*Zizzy Lizzy the Fly*), based loosely on prerevolutionary songs and children's poems, is just one notable example of the cultural continuities that bridged the imperial and Soviet periods in children's literature.

Nature writing formed another through line from the imperial period harking back to Turgenev's 1852 *Sketches from a Hunter's Album*, which melded vivid descriptions of the natural world with socially conscious views of the peasantry and the institution of serfdom. At first glance, the continuation of this tradition after 1917 seems to have little to do with the ideological orientation of the Soviet project: the writings of Vitaly Bianki and Mikhail Prishvin, two of the best-known nature writers for children of the Soviet era, appear now as endearing educational materials designed to teach children about the natural world. All the same, even nature writers had to adjust their style during the Stalin era in response to the ideological dictates of the times. Bianki's stories "The Owl" (1925) and "The Little Ant Who Hurried Home" (1936), both of which are reproduced here, illustrate this shift. "The Owl" is a classic folktale reflecting the oral tradition and stylized folk meters of the distant past. Like most folktales, it contains a moral—in this case, that everything in nature is connected and the survival of each species depends on maintaining a natural balance. Published over a decade later, "The Little Ant Who Hurried Home" contains no trace of folk motifs: written in accessible, colloquial language, the tale underscores the importance of mutual cooperation, helping others, and the needs of the collective—by then well-worn socialist messages.

Connections to the imperial past became increasingly suspect as the Soviet era wore on, and writers who were seen as less than fully committed to the communist cause often suffered dire consequences. The fact that Chukovsky and Marshak survived the Stalin era despite their prerevolutionary roots and clear European influences tells us more about the importance of proximity to power than it does about their aesthetics. Marshak and Chukovsky, who would go on to earn six Stalin Prizes between them, were state-appointed stewards of the evolving field of Soviet children's literature, recruiting new talent and organizing conferences and events to promote emerging writers. In addition to being talented poets, both challenged the vision of Nadezhda Krupskaya, Lenin's wife, who wanted fairy tales and absurdist works to be excised from the Soviet children's canon due to their connection to the "bourgeois" literary past. Despite Krupskaya's formidable influence, it was Chukovsky's and Marshak's artistic visions, and not Krupskaya's, which were to make a lasting mark on Russian children's writing.

Other writers were not so fortunate. Vvedensky and Kharms were persecuted for their absurdist style and failure to conform to the aesthetics of Socialist Realism. Both were arrested for anti-Soviet activities, Vvedensky in 1941 and Kharms on two occasions a decade apart (in 1931 and 1941). Vvedensky died while being evacuated from Kharkiv during the approach of Hitler's armies, and Kharms died of starvation in 1942 in the psychiatric ward of the Kresty prison during the Siege of Leningrad.[2] Kharms wrote under some ten pseudonyms, making it difficult to fully assess the scope of his contribution to Soviet children's literature.[3] Despite this uncertainty, it is clear that Kharms and other OBERIU poets have had an outsized impact on the development of contemporary Russian children's literature, inspiring the publication of new manifestoes calling for a children's literature grounded in word play, nonsense language, and absurdist aesthetics after the fall of the Soviet state in 1991.

Looking back at the 1920s and early 1930s and at the enormous task of creating a new literature for children during a period of extreme political and economic strife, we are struck by the extraordinary innovation during the first fifteen years of Soviet rule. This body of work was made possible by the establishment of new institutions, one of the first and most notable being Raduga (Rainbow) Publishers in 1922. Despite being founded at the end of a four-year civil war, within several years it was publishing over a hundred children's titles annually, including works by Vladimir Mayakovsky, Daniil Kharms, Samuil Marshak, El Lissitzky, and Osip Mandelstam. Other key institutions established in this

---

2 This era in Soviet history was particularly dangerous for writers, including for children's writers. Lev Kvitko, Matvei Bronshtein, Grigory Belych, and Osip Mandelstam were killed or died in prison, while Nikolai Zabolotsky, Tamara Gabbe, Alexandra Lubarskaya, Yan Larri, and Rady Pogodin were sent to labor camps.

3 Ben Hellman, *Fairy Tales and True Stories: The History of Russian Literature for Children and Young People, 1574–2010* (Leiden: Brill, 2013), 303.

period were children's magazines, such as *Ezh* (short for "monthly journal," also the word for hedgehog) and *Chizh* (an acronym for "extraordinarily interesting journal," also meaning siskin), which were instrumental in distributing new children's works across the vast empire and developing new talent. Another key institution was the Soviet Writers Union, an arm of the Communist Party that served to professionalize the field by providing writers with a regular salary, secretarial support, writers' retreats, childcare, and health services.

By the time the Soviet Writers Union appeared in 1932, a radically new literature for children was flourishing as part of a broader literacy project to educate a new generation of communists. The institutions associated with this endeavor, including libraries, schools, reading circles, and book clubs, expanded exponentially over the course of the 1920s. By the early 1930s, millions of Soviet children were enrolled in state schools, reading and writing in Russian; and in the Soviet Socialist Republics, millions of other children were learning to read and write in their native languages in addition to Russian. With the cornerstone of a new children's literature in place, efforts were accelerated to purge the field of "backward," prerevolutionary writers, which included most of the people working in children's literature at the time, and to recruit "new people." Although some writers survived this transition, many were viewed as expendable reactionaries who had to go.

By the early 1930s, Chukovsky and Marshak were leading the growing children's literature industry, with Maxim Gorky providing a guiding hand. Despite the incredible violence of Stalin's era and World War II, and the difficult conditions for literary production, remarkably talented new figures emerged. Arkady Gaidar, Sergei Mikhalkov, and Agnia Barto, for example, published lasting works for children, among them some of the most beloved children's texts in the Russian language. Although the works of Kharms and Gaidar read like products of different cultural universes, the two were direct contemporaries. This fact demonstrates that the radical change in style from the 1920s to the mid 1930s was not simply the result of generational turnover; rather, it was the effect of an aesthetic sea change. Although Socialist Realism remained the dominant aesthetic to the end of the Stalin era in 1953 (with "realism" being a gross misnomer for the socialist fantasies denoted by this term), many children's writers were able to fashion new heroes under this banner, some with wildly popular appeal. Gaidar's *Timur and His Team* and Mikhalkov's "Uncle Styopa" forged a new mold, with Timur becoming a prototype for ideologically committed youth, and Uncle Styopa becoming a new Soviet Superman. Larger than life, Uncle Styopa eclipsed his American counterpart (who could only "leap tall buildings in a single bound") by helping the sick and downtrodden, thus making him a socialist version of the invincible superhero.

Although there were many women working in the children's literature industry and in the Soviet education system, Agnia Barto was the only woman author to achieve superstar status as a children's writer before the 1970s. This fact is surprising given the large number of high-profile women authors who wrote for children in the West, such as Beatrix Potter, Margaret Wise Brown, Beverly Cleary, Enid Blyton, Judy Blume, and Lois Lowry, to name just a few. Thanks to the professionalization of children's writing in the Soviet era, Barto was able to live by her pen; she became a household name due to frequent appearances on state radio and television, enjoying a long and active career until her death in 1981 at the age of seventy-five. Barto's position as the only prominent woman in the company of men is even more surprising given the Soviets' advocacy of equality between the sexes and efforts to eliminate gender discrimination. Countering dominant narratives of masculine heroism, Barto poeticized family life, everyday events, and the inner world of the child.

In addition to the large number of original works for children published in the USSR, a wide variety of literary translations of children's works appeared in Soviet Russia as well. Some of these works are not direct translations of the original text, but literary adaptations, with liberties taken to alter the tone, plot, and overall message of Western works for young Soviet readers. Some of the best-known literary adaptations of the Stalin era include Aleksey Tolstoy's 1935 *The Golden Key, or the Adventures of Buratino*, adapted from Carlo Collodi's 1883 *Pinocchio* and excerpted in this volume; Alexander Volkov's 1939 *The Wizard of the Emerald City*, based on Frank Baum's 1900 novel *The Wonderful Wizard of Oz*; and Kornei Chukovsky's 1929 *Doctor Ouch-It-Hurts*, adapted from Hugh Lofting's 1920 *Doctor Dolittle*. Today many these works would be considered unlicensed translations, loose borrowings, or even plagiarized texts with no reference being given to the original. However, adapting Western works was considered a legitimate form of textual production in the USSR given the lack of attention to international copyright.[4]

With the end of the Stalin era, Khushchev's Thaw in the late 1950s and 1960s sparked a welcome revival in children's literature and culture. Following the terror of Stalin's purges and the loss of 26 million Soviet citizens during World War II, the Thaw marked a turn away from monumental heroism and toward everyday concerns and the lives of ordinary people. This shift occurred in recognizably gendered terms as a move away from the masculinized hero toward a feminization of culture with an emphasis on domestic life, emotions, and everyday acts

4 See Hellman, 253, 312–313, 421–424.

of kindness. This shift was reflected in literary genres as well, with children's poetry experiencing a resurgence during the Thaw. Poets like Boris Zakhoder, Genrikh Sapgir, Emma Moshkovskaya, Irina Pivovarova, and Oleg Grigoriev conveyed children's inner lives in innovative meters and rhymes, echoing the aesthetic of the OBERIU poets. The Thaw was also more welcoming of women writers, including Alexandra Brushtein, Irina Tokmakova, and Renata Mukha, among others.

Children's prose was likewise transformed during the Thaw period as new writers entered the field and privileged new genres. The social fairy tale, such as Veniamin Kaverin's "The Sandglass" and "Many Good People and One Envious One" (excerpted in this volume) and the philosophical fairy tale both took center stage as modern variants of a centuries-old form. Such works took an ironic or satirical view of monumental human projects, emphasizing instead the everyday joys of friendship, small-scale adventures, and acts of compassion. If the heroes of the Stalin era were larger than life, then the protagonists of the Thaw period were small, unremarkable creatures whose lives and adventures were familiar to those of their readers. The most famous philosophical fairy tale of the period, Sergei Kozlov's "Hedgehog in the Fog" (1975), included in this volume, inspired the eponymous film animated by Yury Norshtein. Both are now modern classics, with the film winning more accolades and international film prizes than any other cinematic production of the Soviet era.

Prose fiction from the Thaw tended to focus on friendships, family, and institutional life. Protagonists like Viktor Dragunsky's Denis from the popular series *The Adventures of Deniska* (1958–1964) were regular kids whose world revolved around relationships and school. Other writers like Alexander Raskin, Viktor Golyavkin, and Nikolai Nosov produced main characters whose humorous antics provided a welcome counterweight to the tragic martyrdom of the previous era.[5] These postwar developments were not limited to the Soviet context: chapter books published in the West in the same period reflect a similar direction, with Beverly Cleary's Ramona Quimby series and Judy Blume's books about ordinary children representing a global shift in portrayals of child subjectivity. Alexandra Brushtein's *The Road Goes into the Distance* (1956–1959, excerpted in Volume 2) was a pivotal work in the Soviet context for its depiction of the inner life of its heroine, Sasha Yanovskaya. Although Soviet children's literature evolved within its own ecosystem, it is becoming increasingly clear that postwar cultural developments in the USSR reflected global processes thanks to

5 Of the four authors, only Nosov is not represented in this anthology. His heir (who is the current copyright holder of his works) did not grant permission for his works to be translated.

increasingly permeable boundaries. Russian translations of J. D. Salinger's *The Catcher in the Rye* and Harper Lee's *To Kill a Mockingbird* were highly influential in the Soviet Union, as were underground translations (samizdat) of C. S. Lewis's *The Chronicles of Narnia.*

The Soviet 1960s likewise ushered in a new era of science fiction, represented most notably by the Strugatsky brothers. It was in this period that sci-fi for children gained increasing popularity, growing out of a long tradition of fantasy literature. In 1965, Kir Bulychev (the pen name of Igor Mozheiko) published his wildly popular novel, *The Girl for Whom Nothing Goes Wrong,* setting the scene for the development of a new kind of children's sci-fi. In the more than two dozen books in this series, Bulychev chronicles the adventures of Alisa, a time-traveling heroine named after his daughter, who journeys to the distant past as well as to Soviet Russia from the late twenty-first century. Through Alisa, readers are introduced to deep space, the bottom of the ocean, and myriad periods of world history. One striking aspect of Alisa is that she grew up with her readership: initially a preschool child, Alisa matured as the series unfolded, appearing as a teenager in later works. Although her adventures were anything but ordinary, her relatability resonated with readers and reflected the tendency to redefine heroism during the Thaw.

Even before the advent of perestroika and glasnost in the mid 1980s, some of the more nonsensical aspects of Soviet life were entering children's literature in the form of social critique. Children's writers like Grigory Oster and Mikhail Yasnov, who were well established by the 1980s, and up-and-coming writers like Andrei Usachev and Sergei Sedov marked the return of the absurd in children's literature. As it had seven decades earlier, the appearance of absurdist elements signaled a societal rupture, this time between the late Soviet era and the tumultuous times that would follow the dissolution of the USSR in December 1991. Given the chaos and multiple economic crises of the 1990s, it is no wonder that the development of original children's literature stalled, as a flood of translated works began entering the country. This wave of translation brought many international children's works to Russian readers, particularly translations of British, American, French, German, Italian, and Swedish originals, now connecting the Russian-speaking world to a global cultural sphere in earnest. Renowned works like J. R. R. Tolkien's *The Hobbit* and *The Lord of the Rings,* Tove Jansson's Moomin series, and newer series by Philip Pullman and J. K. Rowling entered Russia and radically changed the cultural landscape for children. This flow was largely unidirectional: Russian children became exposed to works from other cultures, while children abroad knew little of Russia's prodigious output of literature for children.

As the old Soviet publishing houses were privatized and new, smaller publishing houses began to emerge, authors like Ekaterina Murashova, Dina Sabitova, Narine Abgaryan, and Mariam Petrosyan continued writing, bringing some of the plots, tropes, and narrative themes from the Soviet period into the post-Soviet era, while at the same time transforming structures and making them relevant for contemporary child readers. Abgaryan's *Semion Andreich* pays homage to Uncle Fedya, the beloved hero of Eduard Uspensky's 1970s series *Uncle Fedya, His Dog, and His Cat.* In a similar vein, Abgaryan's wildly popular Manyunya series echoes Dragunsky's *The Adventures of Deniska,* updating the plot with two mischievous girls who are best friends. The nostalgic nod to Soviet children's classics at once underscores the cultural roots of the first wave of post-Soviet children's writers, while also signaling that its Soviet-era roots had not yet been severed.

More recent texts by contemporary authors like Artur Givargizov, Mikhail Esenovsky, Masha Rupasova, and Anastasia Orlova exhibit new attitudes toward the child reader, abandoning the didacticism of the Soviet era while echoing the linguistic experimentation and wordplay of the 1920s. The parallels between the Soviet 1920s and the present era remind us that is it insufficient to point to generic "Soviet" influences when trying to better understand the contemporary moment. Today's writers are cognizant of the extraordinary variety of authors, works, and contexts that comprise their literary heritage, including children's literature from the imperial period. The fact that so many contemporary writers are finding inspiration in the Soviet 1920s underscores the deep connection between political change, formal experimentation, and cultural renewal, both then and now.

In the hundred-year period represented in this anthology, we see two very different, yet deeply connected processes of cultural renewal reflected in literature for children: the first following the Bolshevik Revolution of 1917, and the second following the end of the Soviet Union in 1991. In both cases, we see children's writers responding to political rupture by integrating the past with the present, sometimes in self-conscious ways. At other times, we see writers from both periods abandoning the past to create something "completely new." Meanwhile, children perceive these complicated processes of cultural transmission as simply a part of their world.

One such snapshot of a child's world appears in Mikhail Yasnov's 1965 "Counting-Rhyme":

> Bucket with a hole for nails,
> picture of the fearless leader,
> shady courtyard, brand-new walls,

morning sun outside the window,
winter smell of New Year candles,
Levitan's astounding bass,
"Monday's child is fair of face,"
clover strewn across the leas,
sounding out the gro-cer-ies,
noise and honks, the Red Square bell,
the physics trick with cork and water,
paperweight and blotting pad,
Pushkin's fairy tales, Zhitkov,
Marshak, Nosov, Mikhalkov,
sun on desks, red banner, school,
tango, gramophone (old-school),
ringing bounce of rubber balls,
Childhood, ashes, down it falls![6]

This concise depiction of childhood during the Thaw seamlessly brings together the physical and natural worlds into a harmonious whole, weaving together cultural threads of holiday rituals, school traditions, symbols of state power, literary figures from the imperial and Soviet periods, and everyday objects. The resulting sense of community and connection, comfort and home, is what gives texts for children their enduring appeal.

The texts that follow depict children's worlds as imagined by thirty-seven authors writing in a unique and dramatic period of human history. Reading these texts through the prism of the present, we see the arc of the Soviet experiment and its eventual end, followed by attempts to recast the experience of childhood, once again, for a new generation of readers. While the cultural specificity of place and time shines through these texts, so too does the universal and fleeting adventure of being a child. We hope that these works will reach a broad range of readers—historians, literary scholars, teachers, children's literature enthusiasts, parents, and of course, children—who seek a bridge to this complicated era and to texts that continue to bring it to life.

—Olga Bukhina, Kelly Herold,
and Andrea Lanoux
September 2024

6 Translation by Olga Bukhina and Ainsley Morse.

PART 1

For Fun and Education (1917–1932)

KORNEI CHUKOVSKY (1882–1969) is one of the best known and most influential figures in Soviet children's literature. Along with Samuil Marshak, Chukovsky created the institutional foundation for the new Soviet children's literature in the early twentieth century. He was born in St. Petersburg, where he set his first narrative poem for young children, "The Crocodile," published just before the 1917 Revolution. Chukovsky subsequently published "Gottascrub" and "Roach the Terrible" in 1923; "Zizzy Lizzy the Fly" in 1924; "Barmaley" in 1925; "Telephone" and "Old Theodora's Trouble and Horror" in 1926; and "Doctor Ouch It Hurts" in 1929. These poems instantly became an integral part of the Soviet children's canon and never fell out of favor, despite intense political criticism by Nadezhda Krupskaya, Vladimir Lenin's wife, and others beginning in the 1920s and continuing into the 1940s. Chukovsky's poems continue to be published today and remain as popular as they were during the Soviet era. Chukovsky's literary work was not limited to his poetry for children: he also translated many British and American authors into Russian, including Mark Twain, Oscar Wilde, and Rudyard Kipling. Chukovsky wrote several influential works on literary theory and translation, and a collection of essays on the development of speech in children, *From Two to Five* (1928). One of his signature projects, a children's Bible titled *The Tower of Babel,* which he had hoped to publish in the USSR, was slated to come out in 1968, but all printed copies were destroyed. "Roach the Terrible" (1923), one of Chukovsky's most famous poems, has sparked discussions about its possible political connotations which continue to the present day. The poem was illustrated by many artists, including **Vladimir Konashevich** (1888–1963), who produced numerous versions for various editions of this popular poem for young readers.

Kornei Chukovsky, *Roach the Terrible*, illus. Vladimir Konashevich (Leningrad: Detizdat, 1935). Courtesy of Columbia University Libraries.

Roach the Terrible

Translated by Anna Krushelnitskaya

Part I

Bears go biking! Biking bears
Ride in singles, ride in pairs!

Next, a cat comes on their heels,
Doing cartwheels on the wheels!

Then mosquitoes at high noon
Fly in on an air balloon!

Crayfish come in from the bog,
Riding on a hobbling dog.

Wolves come riding on a mare,
        Bunnies pile on with no fare
In a streetcar, lions zoom
In a taxi off the road,
And behind them comes a toad
        Riding on a broom.

They ride, they laugh and giggle,
They snack on little cakes.

When, from a dark, dark alley,
Shiny, brown and smug,
Out crawls a cockroach,
A big bad bug!
Roach the Big, Roach the Mean, Roach the Terrible!
Whiskers wiggle on his snout
As he starts to growl and shout:
"Hey, sit tight there! I'll be right there!
I'll be quick to eat you up!
        I'll be quick, I'll be fast, I'll be merciless!"

The creatures shook in fright.
Some passed out like a light.
A wolf and his wolf brother
Swallowed one another.
A baffled alligator
Grabbed a toad and ate her.
Big Mama Elephant gave a whine,
Plopping on a porcupine.

All the beasts got scared but crayfish,
Spunky crayfish who were brave-ish:
Watch their feelers swing and sway
As they go crawling back away,
Gamely shouting at the whiskered bogeyman:
"That's enough with growls and shouts!
We, too, have whiskers on our snouts
And we can wiggle-wag
As much as you can brag!"
So they said as they kept creeping backwards.

Now, Hippo stands up and declares
To alligators, whales, and bears:
"He who stops this awful ravage,
He who fights this awful savage,
He'll get paid for derring-do!
He'll get not one frog, but two!
I'll award him the Pinecone of Glory!"

"We're not frightened, we're not pale!
We will smite him! We won't fail!
We will bite him,
We will fight him,
Tusk and talon, tooth and nail!"

Creatures went on the attack
In a big excited pack.
But when they saw the whiskered snout—
Eek! Eek! Eek!
They went running out, out, out!
Eek! Eek! Eek!
Then, they hid in the woods and sat jiggling,
Terrified of the whiskery wiggling.

Hippo, with an angry face,
Yelled: "For shame! You're a disgrace!
Hey, you rhinos, bulls, and bears!
Come at once out of your lairs.
Up and go!
Fight the foe!
Stab him with your horns!"

But the rhinos, bulls, and bears
Said together from their lairs:
"We would go
And fight the foe,
Our precious hides need saving though.
They, like horns, don't come cheap in this day and age."

They hide behind small shrubs and hills,
Shaking but trying to keep still.
Big elephants crouch in a narrow ditch.
    Gators crawl through the nettles, which makes them itch.
Woods are filled with furry ears quivering
And teeth clacking, as creatures sit shivering.

Wily monkeys start a foot race!
Each one grabs a monkey suitcase.
In a whiff, they're up and gone,
One by one.

The shark was very spry
As she waved her tail goodbye.
The last to go was a cuttlefish:
The cuttlefish
Was a scuttlefish.

Part II

Now the cockroach is king, Roach the Cruel.
Hill and valley are under his rule.
Creatures bow to his whiskers in fright.
(May he rot, the accursed parasite!)
He likes to parade and strut,
Stroking his big glossy gut:
"Beasts! Bring me your littlest baby beasts.
I will feast on your babies for dinner."
Poor beasts, oh, those poor worried beasts!
They howl in each den, in each lair,
They wail and they glare,
They cry and they swear
At the glutton and his horrid feasts.
No beast mother would ever give up
Her kitten, her calf, or her pup,
Her baby, so helpless, so meek,
To a loathsome underfed freak!
Now the heartbroken beasts weep and cry
As they kiss their sweet babies goodbye.

But one early morn, out of the blue,
There came a bouncing kangaroo.
When she saw the whiskered snout,
She giggled as she hopped about:
"So that's your famous monster thug?
Hardee-har!
That is just a dumpster bug!
Hardee-har!
Roach the Plain, Roach the Brown, Roach the Small!
Scrawny Legs! All he can do is crawl!
A louse has you cowed!
Tell me now, are you proud?
You've got claws,
You've got tusks,
You've got jaws!
Tsk-tsk-tsk!
You're so big, he's so small, yet you bowed!"

Hippos whispered, "No-no-no!
Keep it down and go, go, go!
Watch your mouth before you blurt!
Run before we all get hurt!"

Then, something rustled in the hedge:
From beyond the forest's edge,
Valleys wide and rivers narrow
Came a small and plucky Sparrow.
Chitter-chitter-chitter-bop!
Chirrup! Chirrup! Hop, hop, hop!
He came, he saw, he ate the bug.
That was the end of Roach the Thug.
Roach the Terrible got his due,
And the beasts bade his whiskers adieu.

Now the happy beasts unite
In excitement and delight:
Bless the hero, bless the Sparrow,
Bless his valor, bless his might!
A donkey sings the Sparrow's praises
Loud and off-key, as he grazes.
A goat keeps the Sparrow's path cleared:
He sweeps it with his own beard.
The marching band comes:
Rams on drums, rams on drums!
Hornets on cornets,
Tooting!
Magpies on bagpipes,
Hooting!
Bats on the roof have a ball,
Waving kerchiefs, one and all!
And Big Mama Elephant
Danced so hard and elegant
That the pink moon in the sky
Shook loose and tumbled down!
The moon hit Papa Elephant
Before it touched the ground.
Because of that elephant romp,
        They all fished for the moon in the swamp
And then tacked the moon up—which was hard to do!

OSIP MANDELSTAM (1891–1938) was one of the most famous and critically acclaimed poets of the twentieth century. Along with Nikolai Gumilev and Anna Akhmatova, Mandelstam founded and theorized the Acmeist school of poetry. Born in Warsaw to a Jewish family, he published first his volume of poems, *Stone,* in 1916, followed by three other collections in the 1920s. In addition to poetry, Mandelstam authored travel sketches, autobiographical prose, a short novel, and several influential essays, including "Conversation about Dante" (1933). Mandelstam was arrested twice: first in 1934, when he was exiled to Voronezh; and again in 1938, after which he was sent to a gulag in Vladivostok where he died shortly afterward. Mandelstam wrote over a dozen short poems for children, which were published in four picture books between 1925 and 1926: *Primus Stove, Two Trams, Balloons,* and *In the Kitchen.* Critics have speculated that *Two Trams* (1925) alludes to Mandelstam's friendship with Gumilev, who was arrested and executed by the Soviet authorities in 1921. *Two Trams* was illustrated by Boris Ender, and remains an inspiration for contemporary artists, including **Anna Desnitskaya** (b. 1987).

Osip Mandelstam, *Two Trams*, illus. Anna Desnitskaya (Moscow: Samokat, 2015). Courtesy of Samokat Publishing House.

Two Trams[1]

Translated by Eugene Ostashevsky

In one tram park there lived two trams:
Click and Zam.
Every morning they went out
Before dawn.

Sweet street, the mama of all trams,
Winking merrily along with electricity.
Sweet street, the mama of all trams,
Sent street sweepers out on the tracks of the city.

Rattling and clattering over joints on the track
Gave Click a shattering platform-ache.

---

1 Reprinted with permission from *The Fire Horse: Children's Poems by Vladimir Mayakovsky, Osip Mandelstam and Daniil Kharms*, trans. Eugene Ostashevsky (New York: The New York Review Children's Collection, 2017), 18-33.

His lights grew groggy towards the evening:
He forgot his number—wasn't five, wasn't three . . .

A cabman and children go laughing at Click:
"A sleepyhead tram, look!"

"Tell me, conductor, excuse me, driver,
Where is my cousin Zam?
It's by his eyes that I always know him,
By his stooped back and his red platform."

At five corners the street began,
To the city gardens that street ran.
Horses trod all over it with their hooves,
People tramped all over it with their boots.
It sent silver rails racing up ahead:
"What happened to Click? Why is he so late?"

Who's that looking with his lights into the dark?
Click has come to a halt on the bridge.
These lights of many colors, they're watery:
"I am tired, driver, let's go home!"

But Zam spirk-sparks,
He's scattering fireworks!
He doesn't want to go to the park,
He clangs clangier than anybody else.

A clock towers over the train station,
Its face round and aglow.
Two lines go around a plate
Like a black mustachio.

Where trams, clumsy as geese,
Turn around,
Where Zam and the boys
Hang around.

"Here comes a motor van.—
I'm not scared. I'm prepared. I'm tram.—
Do tell me, where's my cousin, where's is my Click?"
"We don't know him,
We never saw him."

"I will ask the horses, the horses,
If they saw an openmouthed tram pass,
Not a trim tram—a traipser, a doofus."
"We don't know him,
We never saw him."

"You tell me, you seven-story
House with the eyes set in stone,
You look out with all your windows
Over all your environs,
What do you know about Click,
The young tram travelling alone?"

The house glared in reply:
"Many of his kind went by!"

"You, my buddies, motorcars,
Admirable for your manners,
Since you always let a tram
Pass before you on the tracks,

Have you heard about Click,
That unhappy vehicle?
He is missing, he's my cousin
With lights that are a pale pink."

"We saw him, we saw him, and we didn't do nothin' to him.
He stands on the square, he himself is a square,
One of his eyes is pink but the other's not there."

"Driver, take me by the hand,
Click is standing in the dark,
Maybe speaking with strange horses,
He is young and a bit thick.
Let us go and meet him, quick!"

And on the square Zam finds Click.

Said one tram to another:
"It's lonely without you, brother!
I am so happy to hear, Click,
When your bells click and clink.
But what happened to your eye? It had a failure.
I'm going to take you in tow. You'll be my trailer.
You're younger, so you get to be the trailer."

VLADIMIR MAYAKOVSKY (1893–1930) was the most famous poet of the early Soviet era, lionized by state authorities in the 1920s. He was born in Baghdadi near Kutaisi, Georgia. Although he wrote only a few children's poems, all were well received by contemporaries. A futurist, a performer, and a visual artist, Mayakovsky wrote and published long poems and poetry collections, satirical plays, movie scripts, propaganda posters, and revolutionary alphabet books for workers accompanied by his own illustrations. He starred in three silent films, was a prominent member of the Left Front of the Arts (LEF), and published a journal with the eponymous title *LEF*. Mayakovsky died by suicide in 1930 at the age of thirty-seven. His most famous children's poems include "The Fire Horse," "Who Could I Be," and "What Is Good and What Is Bad," the last of which was first published in 1925 with illustrations by **Nikolai Denisovsky** (1901–1981) and regularly republished during the Soviet era.

Vladimir Mayakovsky, *What Is Good and What Is Bad*, illus. Nikolai Denisovsky (Leningrad: Rabochee izdatel'stvo "Priboi," 1925). Courtesy of Princeton University Library.

What Is Good and What Is Bad

Translated by Ainsley Morse

A teeny son
                    was wondering
and had to ask his dad:
"Tell me please, pop:
                    what is good
and also, what is
                    bad?"

I'll tell you
          straight, my little ones—
come and have a look—
what that dad
                    told his son
is going in
                    this book.

"If the wind's
                    all raging wild,
if the
          thunder's rolling—
everybody understands
                    that's hardly
good for
                    strolling.

A little drizzle
                    —now it's gone.
There's sun
          all over now.
This
          is very, very good
for all folks, big
                    and small.

If
your kid
is foul as mud
all smudged from eyes
to chin—
clearly
this
is very bad
for your children's skin.

If
a boy
just loves his soap
and toothpaste makes him sing,
such a boy
is very sweet,
doing the right thing.

If a
rotten ruffian
beats a fragile youngster,
I don't even
want to see him
here inside
my book, sir.

This one here yells:
'Don't you dare
hit kids
who are more slight!'
This boy here's
so good, I swear,
He's just a splendid sight!

If you
tear up books and balls
one after the
other,
the Octobrist Scouts will howl:
that one's not our brother.

If a boy
works night and day
and chooses
books,
not toys,
in this book
we write: hurray!
now there's
a real good boy.

Here's a squirt who's
on the run
afraid of an old crow.
Boys like that
are chicken-livered.
And that's
a bad way to go.

This one,
though he's just knee-high,
takes on
that silly bird.
What a brave boy!
Very good—
in life
you're undeterred.

This one's
crawled in mud
and glad
that his shirt's all mucky.
Kids like that,
they say,
are bad,
or even yucky.

This one
	cleans up
by himself—
	washes
		his galoshes.
He's a good one,
	that's for sure
although he's very small.

Every son,
	remember
		this;
every kid
	should know:
	from every son
	that is
		a piglet
a pig will
	surely grow."

	The little boy
	went off, so glad,
deciding as he should:
"I'll never
	do things that are b a d ,
	only that are
		g o o d ."

VITALY BIANKI (1894–1959) was born in St. Peterburg. Bianki was a soccer player, a mathematician, and a member of the Socialist Revolutionary Party before becoming a museum director, a schoolteacher, and the best-known nature writer for children during the Soviet era. His first story, "The Red Sparrow's Travel," was published 1923 in the children's magazine *Sparrow*. Bianki was arrested and exiled several times, although he was able to return to his home city of Leningrad with the help of Maxim Gorky and his wife, Ekaterina Peshkova. Bianki wrote over three hundred short stories, novellas, and articles about nature. His work appeared in various collected volumes, newspapers, encyclopedias, and picture books from the mid 1920s to the present day. His short story "The Owl" (1925) is written in the style of a traditional Russian fairy tale, and is one of the earliest examples of ecological writing for children in Russian.

The Owl

Translated by Andrea Lanoux

An Old Man sat drinking tea. Not plain tea, but tea with milk. Along came an Owl.

"Greetings, my friend!" said the Owl.

The Old Man replied: "Well now, Owl, with the daring crown, pointy ears and crooked beak. You run from the sun and shun people. What friend are you to me?"

The Owl became cross.

"Fine then, you old Geezer!" she said. "I won't fly over your meadow at night and hunt your mice. Catch them yourself."

The Old Man said, "Ha! So this is how you threaten me? Scram while you still can!"

The Owl flew away and settled in the hollow of an oak tree.

Night came. The mice called out to one another from their burrows in the Old Man's meadow.

"Say, pal, have you seen the Owl with the daring crown, pointy ears and crooked beak?"

A Mouse squeaked to another in reply: "Neither feather nor screech from the Owl! Now we are free without fetters, we can frolic in the meadow!"

The mice skipped out of their holes and scampered across the field.

The Owl called out from the hollow:

"Ha-ha, Old Man! Look, the mice are out, and worse it will get. They say they're on the prowl."

"Let them prowl," said the Old Man. "Mice aren't wolves, they won't eat the cows' hooves."

The mice were riffling through the dirt, digging up earth, looking for bumblebee hives, and hunting bees alive.

Again the Owl called out from the hollow:

"Ha-ha, Old Man! Look, and worse it is: your bees have all flown the coop!"

"Let them fly away," said the Old Man. "What use are they to me? No wax and no honey—only stings and no money."

A clover field was blooming in the meadow, heavy with flowers reaching to the ground. But the bumblebees had flown away, paying the clover no mind and taking no pollen from flower to flower.

The Owl called out from the hollow:

"Ha-ha, Old Man! And you thought it couldn't get any worse: now you have to take the pollen from flower to flower yourself."

"The wind will take it," said the Old Man, scratching the back of his head.

Just then a wind blew through the meadow, knocking the pollen to the ground. The pollen did not make it from flower to flower, so clover will no longer grow in the meadow. This bothered the Old Man.

The Owl called out from the hollow:

"Ha-ha, Old Man! Your cow is bellowing, begging for clover. They say hay without clover is like porridge with no taste."

The Old Man was silent.

The cow had been fit as a fiddle from the clover, but now that was all over. When it came time to milk the cow, her milk was ever thinner.

The Owl called out from the hollow:

"Ha-ha, Old Man! Didn't I tell you, you would bow to me?"

The Old Man cursed, but it was no matter. In the hollow sat the Owl, not catching mice. The meadow was overtaken with mice looking for bumblebee nests. The bees flew off to other meadows, leaving the Old Man's meadow fallow. The clover in the meadow refused to grow in, and the cow without clover grew scrawny and thin. The cow began to give little milk, and plain tea was of not the Old Man's ilk.

With nothing to put in his tea, the Old Man gave in to the Owl:

"Okay you, Owly-Prowly, help me out of this pickle now. I have no milk for my tea."

From the hollow, the Owl batted her big round eyes and tapped her sharp talons: flitter-flutter, rap-tap.

"There you go now, Old Chap," she said. "Quit the ill will and try to be nice. You think it's easy for me without your mice?"

The Owl forgave the Old Man, then she sprang from the hollow and flew out to the meadow to scare off the mice.

The Owl went out to catch mice.

The mice hid in their holes from fright.

The bumblebees buzzed over the meadow, taking the pollen from flower to flower.

The clover covered the meadow with a reddish hue.

The cow went to the meadow to eat the clover.

The cow grew heavy with milk.

And once again the Old Man began to drink his tea with milk. He sang the Owl's praises, bid her visits, and showed her the greatest respect.

SAMUIL MARSHAK (1887–1964), is widely known as one of the two founders of Soviet children's literature, along with Kornei Chukovsky. Marshak was born in Voronezh. He began his career as a poet with his first volume of verse, *Zionedes*, published in 1907 in St. Petersburg. In 1920, he founded the first Soviet theater for children in Ekaterinodar. After returning to Leningrad in 1923, Marshak was involved in the establishment of a number of children's magazines, including *New Robinson, Siskin,* and *Hedgehog*. He played an integral role in the Leningrad division of the children's publishing house Detgiz, where the works of many important poets and writers were first published. In 1937, at the height of Stalin's purges, Detgiz was almost closed for political reasons, and several of Marshak's close colleagues were fired or arrested. After these events, Marshak left Detgiz and moved to Moscow, where he continued to promote Soviet children's literature. Over the course of his career, he received four Stalin State Prizes, a Lenin Prize, and two Orders of Lenin. Marshak wrote numerous poems, fairy tales, and plays for children. He was also a prolific translator of English poetry, including that of William Shakespeare, Robert Burns, William Blake, Edward Lear, Robert Louis Stevenson, Rudyard Kipling, and A. A. Milne. He also translated many traditional English and Scottish ballads and nursery rhymes. Marshak continued to work as a journalist throughout his life, and published works of literary criticism in addition to his own lyric poetry. Marshak's early poems for children, "Circus" (1924), "Ice Cream" (1925), and "Baggage" (1926), were illustrated by the renowned artist **Vladimir Lebedev** (1891–1967), and are now classics of Soviet children's literature.

Samuil Marshak, *Baggage*, illus. Vladimir Lebedev, in *Fairytales. Songs. Riddles*, ed. S. Marshak (Moscow-Leningrad: Detgiz, 1953).

Baggage

Translated by Eugene Ostashevsky

A lady was checking her baggage:
        One sofa,
        One suitcase,
        One package,
One picture, one spatula, four pierogi,
And one teeny-weeny doggy.

This lady received at her station
All the relevant documentation—
Four green tags in exchange for her baggage:

Her sofa,
Her suitcase,
Her package,
Her picture, her spatula, her pierogi,
And her teeny-weeny doggy.

Porters to the railcar go,
Loading up the rail cargo.
There, it's packed, that baggage:
The sofa,
The suitcase,
The package,
The picture, the spatula, the pierogi,
And the teeny-weeny doggy . . .
But, as the train was about to depart,
The puppy jumped out of the car.

After several stops, a big scare:
One of the items is not there!
They nervously count the baggage:
One sofa,
One suitcase,
One package,
One picture, one spatula, four pierogi . . .
"Comrades! Where's the doggy?"

By the door there chanced to occur
A huge cur with bristling fur.
"Catch it! Catch it!" "Into the baggage
Hold it!"—Next to the package,
The picture,
The four pierogi . . .
Right where they once had the doggy.

When it came time to get off
At a difficult to pronounce stop,
They carried toward her carriage

Every piece of the lady's baggage:
    The sofa,
    The suitcase,
    The package,
The picture, the spatula, the pierogi . . .
In the back on a leash came the doggy.

The dog grrrrrrrrrowls,
The lady hooooooooowls:
"Criminals! Thieves! Scoundrels!
Why did you bring me that mongrel?"
She hurled aside her package,
She kicked aside her baggage,
    Her picture,
    Her spatula,
    Her pierogi . . .
"Just give me back my doggy!"

"Madam, calm down. At your station
Of origin—says the documentation—
You checked in the following baggage:
    One sofa,
    One suitcase,
    One package,
    One picture,
    One spatula,
    Four pierogi,
And one teeny-weeny doggy.
    However,
    While left on its own,
    Your dog
    Appears to have grown!"

DANIIL KHARMS (Daniil Yuvachev, 1905–1942) was born in St. Petersburg. An avant-garde poet, playwright, and member of the Leningrad artistic collective known as OBERIU (The Union of Real Art), Kharms wrote extensively for children, in part because he was not able to publish his works for adults under Soviet censorship. As a children's writer, Kharms collaborated with *Siskin*, *Hedgehog*, and other magazines for young readers, where he published under various pseudonyms, answered readers' questions, and contributed an astonishing array of absurdist poetry for children. During his short life, Kharms published six collections of children's poetry. He was detained in 1931 and exiled to Kursk for introducing *zaum* (nonrational experimental language) into children's literature as a way to obscure his anti-Soviet ideas. After a second arrest in 1941 for allegedly distributing German propaganda, Kharms died in a prison hospital. Kharms's poetry was rediscovered in the 1960s, having disappeared from publication for several decades; readers encountered it first in samizdat (self-published journals and books) and then gradually in print publications. His work has experienced a strong revival in the post-Soviet era, making him one of the most reprinted children's authors since 1991. His poems, "Mr. Golden Samovar" and "Ivan van Littleaxe," were published in 1929, the first of which was illustrated by **Vera Ermolaeva** (1893–1937).

Daniil Kharms, *Mr. Golden Samovar,* illus. Vera Ermolaeva (Moscow: Gosudarstvennoe izdatel'stvo, 1929). Courtesy of the Russian State Children's Library.

Mr. Golden Samovar

Translated by Ilya Bernstein

Have you ever seen a SAM?
Have you ever seen an O?
Have you ever seen a VAR?

Have you ever,
Have you ever
Seen a Russian SAMOVAR?

Mr. Samovar was Stately.
Mr. Samovar was Plump.
Not just chubby,
Not just tubby,
Not just fat—
But Stately Plump!

Boiling water was inside,
Splish-and-splashing was inside,
Swish-and-swooshing was inside!
All a-steaming and a-huffing,
All a-huffing and a-puffing,
Boiling water coming out,
Coming out—
Through the spout!

Bright and early in the morning
Uncle Petya came downstairs.
Bright and early,
Bright and early
Uncle Petya came downstairs.

"I could use a cup of tea!"
"Yes, I could!" said Uncle Petya.
"Yes, indeed!" said Uncle Petya,
"I could use a cup of tea!"

After him came Auntie Katya,
Auntie Katya with her cup.
With her beautiful,
Her precious,
Her exquisite little cup.

"As for me," said Auntie Katya,
"If you please," said Auntie Katya,

"To be sure," said Auntie Katya,
"I require a cup of tea."

In walked Grandpa in his slippers,
In walked Grandma with her cane.
In walked Grandpa,
In walked Grandma,
With their slippers and their cane.
"Personally," Grandpa said,
"What I really want is tea.
What I really,
What I really,
What I REALLY want is tea."

"I could also," Grandma said,
"Drink a little," Grandma said,
"Tea for breakfast," Grandma said.
"May I have a little tea?"

In ran Anya, dressed in red.
"Hello, everyone!" she said.
"Here I am!
Give me tea!
Make it extra sweet for me!"

Then came Moskowitz the cat,
Purry, furry, soft as silk,
For a little,
For a little
Boiling water with his milk.

Do you know what happened next?

Boris, finally, arrived.
Yawning, ya-a-a-awning, he arrived.
Stretching, stre-e-e-etching, he arrived.
Very sleepy he arrived.

Boris rubbed his eyes and said,
"Let me have a cup of tea.
Let me have a—
Let me have a—
Let me have a cup of tea."

Everybody,
Everybody,
Tipped the samovar
Tip tip tip.
But the only thing they got
Was
A tiny
Drip drip drip.

Mr. Russian Samovar!
Mr. Golden Samovar!
Mr. Empty Samovar!

Mr. Samovar has nothing
For a lazy lazybones,
Mr. Samovar has nothing
For a sleepy sleepyhead!
Not a drip drip,
Not a drop drop,
For a sleepy sleepyhead!

Ivan van Littleaxe[2]

Translated by Ainsley Morse

Ivan van Littleaxe went out on a hunt,
his poodle came too, jumping over the fence.
Ivan fell into the swamp like a log,
and the poodle sank into the creek like an axe.

---

2 Translator's note: "Ivan" is pronounced *Aye-van* in the text that follows.

Ivan van Littleaxe went out on a hunt,
his poodle came too, hopping just like an axe.
Ivan plopped over the swamp like a log,
and the poodle jumped over the fence in the creek.

Ivan van Littleaxe went out on a hunt,
his poodle fell into the fence in the creek.
Ivan just like a log jumped right over the swamp,
and the poodle a-hopping fell onto an axe.

ALEXANDER VVEDENSKY (1904–1941) was born in St. Petersburg, and became a prominent member of the Leningrad OBERIU group. Like his close friend Daniil Kharms, Vvedensky worked in children's literature in part due to the impossibility of publishing his absurdist poems and plays for adults. His children's writings and translations first appeared in *Siskin, Hedgehog,* and other children's magazines in 1928. Vvedensky was extremely prolific and published more than forty children's books of prose and poetry. Many of Vvedensky's children's poems, such as his 1937 "Lullaby" written for his son, had a songlike quality. Like many other writers, Vvedensky was arrested in the early 1930s, after which he was exiled to Kursk. In 1936 he moved to Kharkiv; five years later he was accused of anti-Soviet agitation and arrested a second time. He died in police custody. His poem "Who?" (1928) was first published in *Hedgehog,* and was republished multiple times during the 1930s.

Who?

Translated by Matvey Yankelevich

1
Uncle Boris sighs and says
That
He's really quite distressed
That
Someone knocked three dishes and two bowls
From the table to the floor,
And threw a hammer and a scythe
In the pan of milk, so white.
Maybe it's the gray cat
Who's to blame,
Or else it's the black dog
Who's to blame,
Or else the chickens flew inside
Through the window from outside,
Fat as a treasure chest, the turkey
Might have burst in without a key,
Knocked three dishes and two bowls
From the table to the floor,
And threw the hammer and the scythe
In the pan of milk, so white.

2
Uncle strides into his study,
And he sees there's something funny—
All the papers strewn all over,
And the inkwell's in the corner.

3
Uncle Boris sighs and says
That
He's really quite distressed
That
The whole can of ink he'd filled

Rolls on the floor where it was spilled,
And a wooden pistol's left
On the writing desk instead.
Maybe it's the gray cat
Who's to blame,
Or else it's the black dog
Who's to blame,
Or else the chickens came inside
Through the window from outside,
Fat as a treasure chest, the turkey
Might have burst in without a key,
Spilled the can of ink he'd filled,
Let it roll without a lid,
Left a toy gun made of wood
On the desk where it had stood.

4
Uncle then glanced at the wall
And stared—
Then he fell right off
His chair.
Now the wall's completely bare
and so dull it's hard to bear:
All the pictures have come down,
They lie trampled on the ground.

5
That's when Uncle sighs and says
That
He's really quite distressed
That
Someone took the pictures down,
Left them trampled on the ground
And instead hung up a flute
And a fishing rod, to boot.
Maybe it's the gray cat
Who's to blame,
Or else it's the black dog
Who's to blame,

Or else the chickens from outside
Through the window came inside,
Fat as a treasure chest, the turkey
Might have burst in without a key,
Hung a tin flute on the wall
And a fishing rod. The gall!

6
Uncle Boris sighs,
"To whom does all this stuff belong?"
Uncle Boris says,
"Whose scythe and hammer and fishing rod?"
Uncle Boris sighs,
"Whose toy pistol made of wood?"
Uncle Boris says,
"Whose tin flute?"

7
The gray cat runs off with a whistle,
But doesn't take the wooden pistol.
The black dog takes off at a pace,
Turns his nose up at the place.
And the chickens stay outside
They don't want to come inside.
And the turkey, fat as a treasure chest,
Struts and huffs and puffs his chest—
He wants none of that tin flute,
Nor the fishing rod, to boot.
But on the threshold, look, there's one
Citizen of eight years young.
That eight-year-old citizen walks in—
That boy named Peter Borodin.

8
Let it be printed in our paper
That
We've solved this unsolved caper:
Who
Knocked three dishes and two bowls

From the table to the floor,
Threw a hammer and a scythe
In the pan of milk, so white,
Spilled the can of ink we'd filled,
Let it roll without a lid,
Left a toy gun made of wood
On the desk where it had stood,
Hung a tin flute on the wall
And a fishing rod? The gall!
The gray cat is not to blame,
Not him.
The black dog is not to blame,
Not him.
And the chickens stayed outside,
They had never come inside.
Fat as a treasure chest, the turkey
Had not burst in without a key.
Only Peter Borodin
Got in.
He's the only one,
It's him.
Tell the world that it was Pete
Who left everything so neat.

PART 2

Heroes and Victims (1933–1953)

BORIS ZHITKOV (1882–1938) was born in Novgorod and grew up in Odesa. He was a writer, traveler, shipbuilder, engineer, sea captain, and an explorer; the sea was his primary passion. Zhitkov began writing about his adventures on the advice of his childhood friend, Kornei Chukovsky. Zhitkov published his essays and short stories about animals, people and their vocations, and notable events in the children's magazines *New Robinson, Hedgehog, Siskin, Pioneer,* and *Young Naturalist.* Many of his stories were collected into volumes, including *The Angry Sea* (1924), *Sea Stories* (1925–1937), and *Stories about Animals* (1935). Zhitkov's greatest success as a children's writer was his book *What I Saw,* which chronicles the summer vacations of a curious boy named Pochemuchka (Why-Is-That). Zhitkov also wrote a novel, *Victor Vavich,* about the 1905 Russian Revolution, although it was poorly received during his lifetime. "Yashka" was first published in the newspaper *Lenin's Sparks* in 1927, and later anthologized in many collections.

Yashka [excerpt]

Translated by Ilya Bernstein

I was twelve years old and going to school. One day, during recess, my friend Nikolai came up to me and said:

"How would you like a monkey?"

I thought he was going to play a trick on me, bonk me over the head with something, and then say: "That's a 'monkey.'" I wasn't about to fall for it.

"No, thanks," I said. "I know about those monkeys."

"No," he said. "I mean it. A real monkey. A nice one. His name is Yashka. And my dad is angry."

"At whom?"

"At Yashka and me. He said: whatever you do, just get him out of here. I think your house would be the best place for him."

After school we went to Nikolai's house. I still didn't believe him. Would I really have my own monkey?

"What's he like?" I kept asking.

Nikolai said: "You'll see. Don't be scared. He's small."

He really was small, just as Nikolai said. When he stood up on his hind legs, he wasn't more than twelve inches tall. His face was all wrinkled, like an old woman's. But his eyes were lively and shiny.

His fur was reddish, but his little paws were black. Exactly like human hands in black gloves. He was wearing a blue vest.

Nikolai shouted: "Yashka, Yashka, come here, I'll give you something!"

And he put his hand in his pocket. The monkey started screaming: "Ay ay ay!" and jumped into Nikolai's arms. Nikolai quickly put him under his coat, hugging him to his chest.

"Let's go," he said.

I couldn't believe my eyes. We were walking down the street, carrying something so marvelous, and no one suspected what Nikolai had under his coat.

On the way to my house, Nikolai told me what to feed the monkey.

"Give him whatever you want. He eats everything. He likes sweets. Candy is trouble. If he gets his hands on candy, he'll stuff himself for sure. He likes tea when it's weak and sweet. Put the sugar right in, two lumps. Don't give him any on the side: he'll gobble up the sugar and won't touch the tea."

I was listening and thinking. "I'll let him have three lumps if he wants. He's so nice and small, like a toy person." Then I remembered that the monkey didn't have a tail.

"Did you cut off his tail?" I asked.

"He's a macaque," Nikolai said. "They don't have tails."

When we reached my house, my mother and sisters were eating dinner. Nikolai and I walked in without taking off our coats.

"Guess what we have!" I said.

Everyone turned to look. Nikolai opened up his coat. Before anyone even had time to see anything, Yashka leaped out of Nikolai's arms and onto my mother's head. Then he pushed off with his little feet and landed on top of the cupboard. He ruined my mother's hairdo completely.

Everyone jumped up and started yelling:

"Oh! Who is that? Who is that?"

Meanwhile, Yashka sat down on top of the cupboard and started making faces, smacking his lips and showing his teeth.

Nikolai was afraid that he was going to get scolded and slipped out the door. No one was looking at him in any case. Everyone was watching the monkey. Suddenly, my sisters said in unison:

"He's so cute!"

My mother kept fixing her hair.

"Where did THIS come from?" she said.

I looked around. Nikolai was gone. That meant that I was now the owner. And I wanted to show everyone that I knew just what to do with a monkey. I put my hand in my pocket and shouted, just as Nikolai had done:

"Yashka, Yashka! Come here, I'll give you something!"

Everyone waited. Yashka didn't even look. He just started scratching himself very rapidly with his little black paw.

Until evening, Yashka didn't come down. He kept jumping between places where he was out of reach: from the cupboard to the door, from the door to the wardrobe, from there to the stove pipe.

In the evening, my father said: "We can't leave him like this overnight. He'll turn the apartment upside down."

So, I started trying to catch Yashka. I ran to the cupboard, and he jumped to the stove pipe. I reached for him there with a broomstick, and he jumped on top of the grandfather clock. The grandfather clock wobbled for a second and stopped. Meanwhile, Yashka was already swinging on the curtains. From there, he leaped to a painting that was hanging on the wall, and the painting tipped to the side. I was afraid that he would jump on the chandelier.

But now everyone started running around and chasing Yashka. We threw a ball at him, spools of thread, matchboxes, and finally chased him into a corner.

Yashka pressed against the wall, bared his teeth, and clicked his tongue to scare us. But we threw a wool shawl over him, wound it around him, and wrapped him up.

Yashka thrashed and screamed. But we soon bundled him up so tightly that only his head was showing. He turned his head this way and that, blinked wildly, and looked as if he was about to cry for being treated so unfairly.

Still, we couldn't bundle him up like this every night, could we?

Father said: "Tie him down. Tie his vest to the leg of the table."

I found a rope, felt for a button on Yashka's back, put the rope through the buttonhole, and made a tight knot. Yashka's vest had three buttons on the back.

Then I carried Yashka to the table, just as he was, all bundled up, tied the rope to a table leg, and only then unfurled the shawl.

How he started to jump around! But there was no way he could tear the rope. He screamed and fumed for a while, and then sat down on the floor sadly.

I fetched some sugar cubes from the cupboard and gave them to Yashka. He grabbed a few with his little black paw and stuffed them inside his cheek. This made his whole face look lopsided.

I asked Yashka to give me his paw. He stretched out his little hand to me.

Then I saw how fine his tiny black fingernails were. A little toy hand! I stroked his fingers, thinking: "Just like a little baby." And I tickled the palm of his hand. Meanwhile, the little baby yanked his hand away and—whack!—slapped me across the face. Before I could blink, Yashka had boxed my ears and jumped under the table. He sat there, scowling. Some baby!

But then I had to go to bed, too.

I wanted to tie Yashka to my bed, but my parents wouldn't let me. I kept trying to hear what Yashka was doing, and I kept thinking that I would have to make a little bed for him, so he could sleep like a person and cover himself with a little blanket. He could put his head on a little pillow. I thought about it, and thought some more, and fell asleep.

In the morning, I jumped up and ran over to look at Yashka without getting dressed. Yashka was gone. The rope was still there, and the vest was still tied to the rope, but no monkey. I saw that all three buttons on the back of the vest had been undone. Yashka had unbuttoned the vest, left it tied to the rope, and run off. I started searching around the room in my bare feet. Yashka was nowhere to be found. I got scared. "What if he ran away?" I thought. He'd been with me for less than a day, and he was already gone! I looked on top of the wardrobe, inside the stove—no trace of Yashka.

"If he ran away," I said to myself, "he must be outside. It's freezing cold outside! Poor Yashka, he'll freeze to death!"

I started feeling cold myself. I ran to get dressed. Suddenly, I saw something moving around in my bed. The blanket was wiggling. A shiver ran through me. So, that's where he was! He must have gotten cold sleeping on the floor, broken loose, and climbed into my bed. Deep under the covers. Meanwhile, I had been asleep and didn't know.

Yashka let me pick him up now. He was half-asleep and didn't resist when I put his blue vest back on.

When we sat down for breakfast, Yashka jumped up on the table, looked around, immediately spotted the sugar bowl, stuck his paw inside, and leaped to the top of the door. He jumped so easily that it looked like he was flying, not jumping. Monkeys have fingers on their feet, the same as on their hands, and Yashka could snatch things with his feet. That was what he did. He would sit in someone's arms, like a baby, with his own arms folded, and in the meantime with his foot he would snatch something from the table. He would snatch a knife and start prancing around the room with it. He did this because he wanted people to chase him, so he could run away from them. Yashka was given tea in a glass. He hugged the glass like a bucket, drank, and made smacking noises with his lips. I gave him all the sugar cubes he wanted then.

When I went off to school, I tied Yashka to a door handle. This time, I tied the rope around his waist, so he wouldn't be able to break free. When I came home, as soon as I walked in I saw what Yashka was doing. He was hanging on the door handle and riding the door like a merry-go-round. He would push off from the door jamb and ride to the wall. Then he would shove off from the wall with his little foot and ride back.

When I sat down to do my homework, I sat Yashka down on my desk. He loved to warm himself by the lamp. He dozed like a little old man in the sun, rocking back and forth. Squinting his eyes, he would watch me dip my pen in the inkwell. Our teacher was strict, and I wrote out my composition cleanly. I didn't dry it with blotting paper, because I didn't want to smudge the ink, and left it to dry on its own. When I came back, I saw Yashka sitting on my notebook, dipping his little finger in the inkwell, grunting, and making inky doodles all over my composition. "Why, you little stinker!" I thought. I almost started crying with frustration. I threw myself at Yashka. But what could I do? He jumped on the curtains—and smeared ink all over them. "So, that's why Nikolai's father got mad at him . . ." I thought.

NIKOLAI ZABOLOTSKY (1903–1958) was a poet, writer, and translator, who was close to the poets of the OBERIU group. Zabolotsky was born near Kazan and moved to Moscow in the age of seventeen. He published his stories and poems for children in *Hedgehog* and *Siskin*, and adapted François Rabelais's *Gargantua and Pantagruel* for children. Zabolotsky's poetry of the 1920s and '30s combined deep philosophical writing with parody and the grotesque. Zabolotsky managed to publish some of his works for adults, but in the mid 1930s he became the victim of a political smear campaign. In 1938, he was incarcerated and spent several years in a labor camp; he was later exiled to Karaganda. In 1945, Zabolotsky was allowed to return to Moscow where he was able to write again and publish his work. He translated the Old Slavic epic poem *The Tale of Igor's Campaign* into Russian, and a number of Georgian poems, including Shota Rustaveli's *The Knight in the Panther's Skin*. Zabolotsky died in Moscow from a heart attack. His story "The Tale of the One-Eyed Little Man" was published in 1933.

The Tale of the One-Eyed Little Man

Translated by Ainsley Morse

On a little old chair sits a little old man,
On his head is a wee wooden hat.
He sits there a-rocking all night and all day,
And his slippers a-bouncing away.

He sits on his chair, waves his arms all around,
When a small one-eyed fellow runs up at a bound.

"My dear, what's gone wrong?
Please open your eye!
Why is it all bandaged?" he cried.

Said the one-eyed fellow to the old man:
"My eye's all closed up and my pupil's been whammed.
I was fighting with crow-lady out on the fly,
And she pecked me right in the eye."

At that the old man sent at once for the beetle.
"Fly quick, my dear bug, do not hem, do not haw.
Catch me that crow within fifteen minutes—
We'll try her in a court of law."

That's no gust of wind, no storm on the way,
It's beetle a-flying 'cross swamps to catch crow.
"If you please, lady crow, to appear in the court—
You have only twelve minutes to go."

Twelve minutes fly by, as all in a rush,
Crow-lady flies in, her wings all a-shush,
They sat her right down, with police escort,
For the beetle to write his report.

"Tell us, crow-lady, your last name, please.
Have you lived in these parts for a while?

Why did you peck the little man in his eye?
This is why you are on trial."

The crow-lady said: "But I'm not to blame,
I myself, Lady Crow, am aggrieved:
The one-eyed little man has destroyed my home,
He wrecked my nest, tore it up into pieces."

"Is that so!"
Cried the old man, terribly cross.
"Is that so!"
And his little cap shook on his head.
"Is that so!"
And his steel slippers rumbled like thunder.
"Is that so!"
And the buckles upon them went ringing.

And that no good little liar fell onto his knees,
And his little head bonked on the very cold floor,
And he cried and he pleaded for a very long while,
'Til the court thought forgiveness was called for.

And the little man went to the angry crow-lady,
And he kissed her crow-foot and he gave her his word,
That never and never and never again
Would he touch the nest of any bird.

And now the music started up,
The beetles banging drums with sticks,
And our little man, like a dashing Spaniard,
Showed crow-lady all of his dancing tricks.

* * *

And if it should happen, my boy, that you see
That crow-lady up in her nest in the tree,
And if the young fledglings are there at the edge,
Remember this fable of mine.

I didn't write this tale all on my own,
The old fellow swore it was true—
The very old man who, under glass in the clock,
Swings back and forth all the day through.

"Tick-tock!"
Says the old man under the glass.
"Tick-tock!"
In reply answers the little hat.
"Tick-tock!"
His slippers beat time on the stone.
"Tick-tock!"
Say the buckles, repeating the tone.

May the pendulum swing, may the minute-hand circle.
The funny old man will not run from the clock.
And still, my boy, nasty behavior toward birds
Will cause dreadful sorrows to knock.

Our fields will fall silent, our gardens be stripped,
And there will breed thousands of pests,
And no one will be there to snatch up and peck them
And take them back home to their nests.

And if my tale suddenly turned out to be real,
A little man would come to you, a bandage on his eye,
He'd look at the garden, and shake his small head,
And together you would cry.

MIKHAIL ZOSHCHENKO (1894–1958), a writer, playwright, and translator, was born in St. Petersburg. Zoshchenko served in World War I and the Russian Civil War as a petty officer. He began publishing his short stories in the 1920s as a member of The Serapion Brothers, a prominent literary group founded in Petrograd in 1921. Zoshchenko's satirical short stories were an immediate sensation, earning him state honors in 1939 and in 1946. In the 1930s, he expanded the scope of his work to include the volumes *Youth Restored, The Blue Book,* and *Before Sunrise,* which he envisioned as a trilogy. In his lifetime, these texts appeared only in excerpts. In 1946, The Zhdanov Doctrine sparked a campaign against two literary magazines, *Zvezda* (*Star*) and *Leningrad,* both of which had published the works of Zoshchenko and the poet Anna Akhmatova, who were later accused of "bourgeois individualism." Subsequently, Zoshchenko was expelled from the Writers Union, a blow from which he never recovered artistically. His story "The New Year's Tree," was published in 1933 in the collection *Lyolya and Minka*; "How Lenin Tricked the Police" was published in 1940 in the collection *Stories about Lenin.* It remains unclear whether these stories were intended as propaganda or as a veiled mockery of the regime.

The New Year's Tree[3]

Translated by Anna Krushelnitskaya

Children, this year I turned forty years old. That means I've seen forty New Year's trees in my lifetime. That's a lot!

Well, for the first three years of my life I, perhaps, didn't understand what a New Year's tree was. My mama, perhaps, carried me out in her arms to show it to me. My dark baby eyes probably stared at the bedecked tree without any curiosity.

But by the time I hit the age of five, children, I already had a pretty good idea of what a New Year's tree was.

I just couldn't wait for that fun holiday. I would even crack the door open a little to sneak a peek at Mama decorating the tree.

Now, my sister Lyolya was seven years old at the time. She was an exceptionally spunky little girl.

Once she said to me, "Minka, Mama went into the kitchen. Let's go to the room with the tree and take a peek at what's going on there."

So, my sister Lyolya and I went into the room. We saw that the tree was very pretty. Under the tree, there were presents. On the tree, there were strings of colorful beads, pennants, lanterns, golden nuts, chewy candies called pastilles, and red apples.

My sister Lyolya says, "Let's not look at the presents yet. Instead, let's each eat one pastille."

So, she walks up to the tree, and, in a blink, she eats one piece of candy off the string.

I say, "Lyolya, since you ate this pastille, I'm also going to eat something right now."

So, I come up to the tree and take a small bite out of an apple.

Lyolya says, "Minka, since you took a bite out of an apple, I'm going to eat another pastille, and I'll take this lollipop, too."

---

3 All religious holidays were banned after the 1917 Revolution, including Christmas. New Year's Day, a secular holiday, soon took its place as one of the biggest holidays of the year, with the New Year's Tree replacing the Christmas Tree as its primary symbol.

Now, Lyolya was a tall gangly legged girl. She could reach up high.

She stood on her tiptoes, opened her big wide mouth, and began munching on her second pastille.

I, on the other hand, was a remarkably short boy. I couldn't reach hardly anything, except for that low-hanging apple.

I said, "Since you, big ol' Lyolya, just ate a second pastille, I will take another bite out of this apple!"

Again, I took the apple into my hands and took a tiny bite.

Lyolya says, "Since you took another bite out of the apple, I will no longer stand on ceremony. I will eat a third pastille right now, and I'll also take a walnut and a firecracker, to keep."

I nearly started bawling. That was because she could reach everything, and I couldn't.

I said to her, "You know, you big dumb ol' Lyolya, if I push this chair to the tree, I can also get something other than this apple."

I began dragging the chair to the tree with my skinny little arms, but the chair fell right on me. I wanted to pick up the chair. The chair fell again. It fell down right on the presents.

Lyolya said, "Minka, I think you broke a doll. Yes, you did. You broke off the doll's porcelain arm."

Then, Lyolya and I heard Mama's footsteps, and we ran into the other room.

Lyolya said, "Well, now, Minka, I can't promise that Mama won't spank you!"

I was about to start bawling, but just then the guests arrived. There were many children with their parents.

Mama lit all the candles on the tree, opened the door and said, "Come in, everybody!"

All the children entered the room with the New Year's tree.

Then Mama said, "Let's have each child come up, and I'll give everyone a toy and a treat."

So, the kids started going up to Mama, one by one. She gave each one a toy. Then she took an apple, a pastille and a lollipop off the tree and gave them to each child as well.

All the kids were very happy. Then, Mama took the apple which I'd taken bites from, and said:

"Lyolya and Minka, get over here. Which of you two took a bite out of this apple?"

Lyolya said, "That's Minka's handiwork."

I yanked Lyolya's braid and said, "Lyolya told me to."

Mama said, "Lyolya will stand in the corner with her nose to the wall. As for you, I was going to give you a wind-up toy train. But now I will give it to the boy who almost got the half-eaten apple."

She picked up the toy train and gave it to some four-year-old boy. He began playing with it right away.

I got so mad at the boy that I hit him on the arm with a toy. He started bawling so hard that his mommy picked him up and said:

"From now on, I will never come visit you with my son again."

And I said, "Go ahead and leave so I can keep the train for myself."

The boy's mom was surprised by my words. She said, "I think your boy will grow up to be a highway robber."

Then Mama picked me up and said to the other mom:

"Don't you dare speak of my son that way. You better take your scabby child and never come here again."

The other mom said:

"That's just what I'll do. I'd rather sit on burrs than be a friend of yours."

And then a third mom said, "I'm leaving, too. My little girl deserves better than a doll with a broken arm."

My sister Lyolya shouted, "You can take your scabby child and leave, too. When you do, I'll take the one-armed doll for myself."

Then I shouted from my mother's arms:

"All of you can just leave so we can keep all the toys for ourselves!"

All the guests started to leave.

Mama was surprised to see that we were all alone.

Suddenly, Papa walked into the room.

He said: "This kind of upbringing will be the ruin of my children. I don't want them to fight, argue, and throw out their guests. If they do, the world won't be kind to them, and they will die lonely."

Papa went up to the tree and blew out all the candles. Then he said: "Go to bed right this instant. Tomorrow I'm going to give all of the toys to our guests."

It's been thirty-five years since that day, children, and I still remember that tree like it was yesterday. In the past thirty-five years, children, I have never eaten an apple that wasn't mine, and I've never hit anyone who was weaker than me. My doctors now say that this is why I am such a relatively cheerful and good-hearted person.

How Lenin Tricked the Police

Translated by Anna Krushelnitskaya

When Lenin was twenty-six years old, he was already a well-known revolutionary, and the tsarist government was deathly afraid of him. The tsar ordered that Lenin be thrown in prison. So, Vladimir Ilyich Lenin spent fourteen months in prison.

After that, the police exiled him to Siberia. There, in Siberia, Lenin spent three long years.

He was sent to a tiny far-off village. It was in the middle of the taiga. There was nothing worth seeing there. It did have a small river named Shush. There was also a small forest nearby, but even that didn't have many trees.

But Vladimir Ilyich didn't despair at being kept in that backwoods place. He spent long days working, writing revolutionary books, talking to peasants, and helping them with his good advice.

In his free time Lenin would go hunting with his hound dog, Zhenka, swim, and play chess. He even carved his own chess pieces out of tree bark. He was very good, even fantastic, at carving things out of tree bark.

So, little by little, time kept passing by. Almost three years went by like that. The end of his exile was near.

Vladimir Ilyich began thinking about where he might move next to keep doing his revolutionary work.

But shortly before Lenin's exile was about to end, the police came to the house where he was staying.

They said, "Listen here. We will do a search of this house. If we find anything banned by the tsar's government, then you better watch out. Instead of letting you go, we will keep you in this backwoods village for three more years, at least."

Lenin did have banned books and many revolutionary papers. All of those books and papers were on the bottom shelf of his bookcase.

So, a fat policeman with a mustache took a post by the door to make sure no one entered or left.

The other policeman, shorter than the first, but just as whiskery and mean, walked around the room sticking his nose in every corner.

He searched the desk and the dresser, peeked into the stove, and even bothered to crawl under the bed to see what all was there.

Then, he went up to the bookcase and asked, "What do you keep in this bookcase?"

Lenin said, "I keep my books in this bookcase."

The policeman said, "Well, let me take a look at these books here to see what kind of books they are!"

The policeman stood by that bookcase trying to decide whether he should start searching from the top shelf or the bottom.

Lenin's wife, Nadezhda Konstantinovna Krupskaya, looked at the policeman and thought: "Please let him start searching from the top shelf. It will be good if he starts from the top because he will get tired by the end of the search, and he won't look through the bottom shelf too carefully. It will be bad if he starts from the bottom shelf because that is where we keep banned books among other ones."

Lenin also looked at the policeman and thought the same thing.

Suddenly, Lenin smiled a little at his idea, then he took a chair and pushed it toward the bookcase. He said to the policeman, "What with your short stature, please don't strain yourself reaching up. Feel free to use this chair to begin checking my books."

The short policeman with a mustache thanked the revolutionary for doing him such a courtesy and climbed up on the chair. Now that he was on the chair, it only made sense for him to start with the top shelf. That was exactly what Lenin had wanted.

Lenin looked at the policeman and smiled.

Krupskaya also smiled, seeing how Lenin made the policeman do exactly as he wanted.

And so, the policeman began digging through the top shelves, reading all the titles and shaking out every book. Time went by. There were many books. In three hours' time the policeman had barely made it through four shelves.

He began looking through the fifth shelf, now with less care. That was in part because the fat policeman who stood by the door had begun to sigh and whimper. He even said to his buddy, "This search is sure taking very long. I am tired and I need a snack."

The short policeman said, "We'll go eat soon. This is the last shelf. But there's probably nothing there, since nothing has turned up on this whole bookcase."

The fat policeman said, "We can see that they are hiding nothing. Let's go have a bite."

After barely a look at the bottom shelf, the short policeman said to Lenin, "As it turns out, we found no banned books in your house. I bid you farewell."

And with those words the policemen left.

When the door closed behind them, Vladimir Ilyich and Nadezhda Konstantinovna began laughing joyfully at how easily the policemen had been fooled.

SERGEI MIKHALKOV (1913–2009) was one of the most popular children's writers of the Soviet era. He was born and lived all his life in Moscow. Mikhalkov began his career as a journalist, and in 1935 he published his most famous children's poem "Uncle Styopa." The poem first appeared in *Pioneer*, and was published the same year as a separate volume with illustrations by Aminadav Kanevsky. The poem was edited many times in subsequent years; the text that follows is a translation of the 1957 edition. "Uncle Styopa" was illustrated by many different artists in the Soviet era, including **V. Moroz**, whose black-and-white illustrations appeared in 1940. Mikhalkov wrote several sequels to "Uncle Styopa," including "Uncle Styopa, Militiaman" (1954) and "Uncle Styopa and Yegor" (1968). Thanks to the poem's enormous popularity, statues of Uncle Styopa were built in Moscow, Prokopyevsk, Nizhny Novgorod, and Samara. Mikhalkov published multiple collections of children's poems and over two hundred satirical fables. His prose for children includes the novella *Feast of Disobedience* (1971), which inspired a Hungarian musical in 1976, and a Soviet animated film in 1977. In the 1960s, Mikhalkov became a public promoter of Soviet literature domestically and abroad, chairing both the Soviet Writers Union and the Moscow Writers Union. Throughout his literary and public career, Mikhalkov was always embraced by the authorities: he received multiple state honors and prizes from various state leaders, from Stalin to Putin, including the Hero of Socialist Labor honorable title, four Orders of Lenin, three Stalin Prizes, a Lenin Prize, and a USSR State Prize, as well as several international awards. Not coincidentally, Mikhalkov also wrote the lyrics for the Soviet and Russian national anthems.

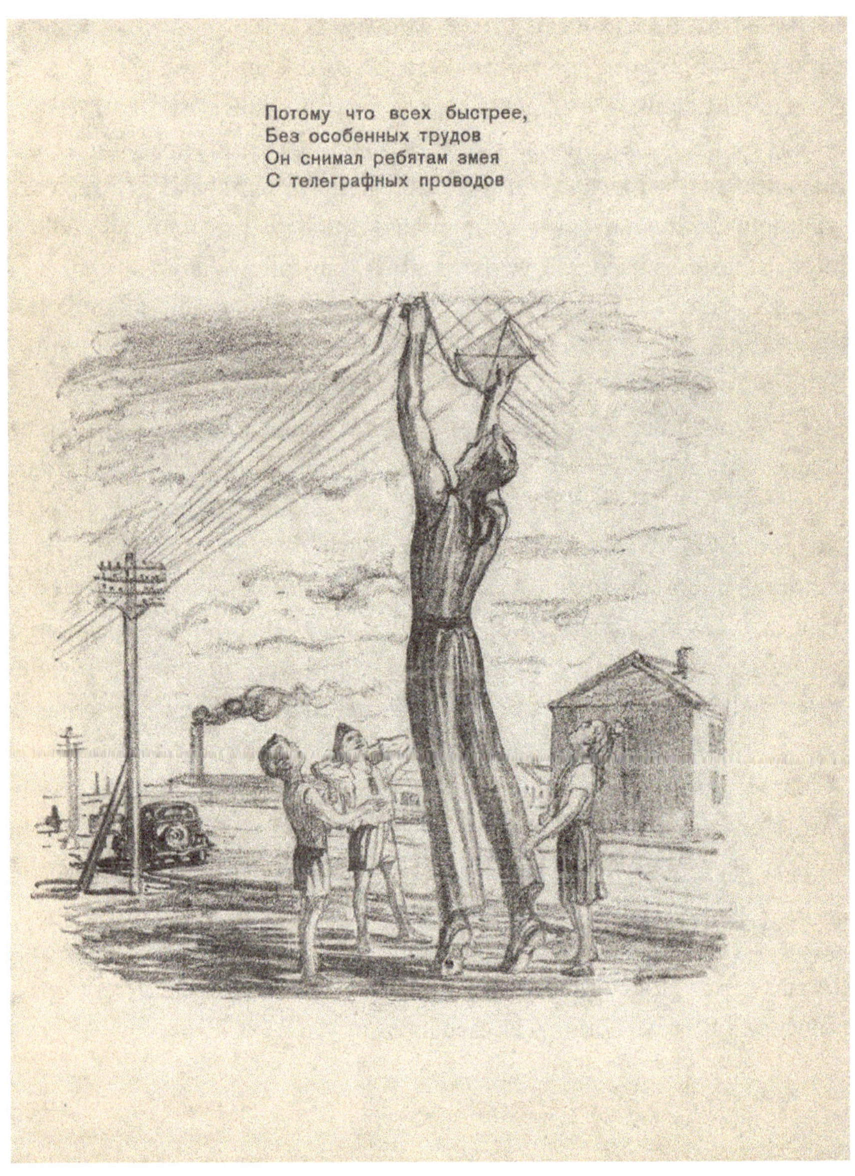

Sergei Mikhalkov, *Uncle Styopa*, illus. V. Moroz (Moscow: Detizdat, 1940). Courtesy of Columbia University Libraries.

Uncle Styopa

Translated by Jamie Olson

Down the street from Lenin's Gate,
in building number 8 slash 1,
lived a person of great height,
known as "Watchtower" to some.

Stepanoff was his family name,
his first name was Stepan,
and of all the local giants,
he was by far the biggest one.

Uncle Styopa, as we called him,
stood tall over everyone.
On his way from work each day,
he could be seen for miles away.

Styopa's two colossal feet
measured out his jaunty stride.
He bought his boots about as big
as you can find: size twenty-five.

At the market, he would seek out
shoes so huge you can't believe it,
and after that he'd have to find
pants that were absurdly wide.

Yet he'd buy these things with gloom:
later, in the mirror at home
he would see the tailor's work—
seam by seam—first split, then burst!

From the road into the yard,
he saw over every fence.
Then the dogs would start to bark:
a thief, they thought, was climbing in!

In the lunch hall, Uncle Styopa
always got a double scoop.
Too long-legged for his bed, he'd
have to rest his feet on stools.

From his chair, he'd reach for books
high up on shelves. At shows, they'd yell,
"Comrade, please sit on the floor!
You can still see fine from there!"

But he always got to go
into stadiums for free:
they would look at him and guess
that he must be the MVP.

Yes, from one end to the other,
the whole neighborhood could say
where Stepanoff worked, as well as
how he lived
and spent his days,

since, much easier and quicker
than anybody else nearby,
he could grab the children's
kites caught in the telegraph lines.

At parades, he'd gladly lift up
anybody who was short,
because each and every person
should admire their nation's troops.

All of us loved Uncle Styopa,
we respected Uncle Styopa:
you couldn't find a better friend
to all the children in our town.

Sometimes, when he hurried home,
the kids would shout, "Hey, how's it goin'?"
And if he sneezed, they'd all respond,
"Bless you! Bless you, Uncle Styopa!"

Uncle Styopa woke up early,
jumped right out of bed,
flung the bedroom window open,
and took a nice cold bath.
Styopa had the cleanest teeth;
he would never skip a brushing.

Sitting in a saddle, his feet
dragging low along the asphalt—
there goes Uncle Styopa riding
on a donkey down the street.
Folks would shout to him, "Hey, buddy,
a camel—that is what you need!"

So he set off on a camel,
and the people shook with laughter,
"Now where are you headed, comrade?
You could crush that sorry creature!
Tall as you are, you should ride
on an elephant instead!"

Uncle Styopa had two minutes
left until he had to jump;
he was feeling kind of nervous
standing on the airplane's ramp.
"Scared of heights," the people laughed,
"The guy's afraid to parachute!"

At the shooting gallery,
Uncle Styopa ducked inside.
He cleared his throat. "Pardon me,
I would like to pay to shoot.
In fact, I want to try my hand
at that bird and that balloon!"

The attendant glanced around
and said to him with some alarm,
"You can play, comrade, but only
kneeling. Otherwise, you might

reach your hand out just to plunder
loot—without a single shot!"

Till the morning in the park,
cheer and merriment would reign,
festive music would ring out—
all the crowd was having fun.

At the entrance, Styopa said,
"I came here for the carnival.
I'd like a mask to hide my face
so no one knows it's me at all."

Then they told him, with a smile,
"Everyone will see it's you!
The town knows you by your size.
Friend, you're absolutely huge!"

Now what's happened?
What's that shouting?
"It's a kindergartner drowning!
Poor boy, he fell from a cliff
into the river. Help the kid!"
As the crowd looked on in wonder,
Uncle Styopa braved the water.

"This is really quite amazing!"
from the bridge they yelled to him.
"Man, for you, the deepest places
only come up to your hips!"

Alive and well, the lucky lad
climbed out safely onto land.

Uncle Styopa, this time around,
saved a boy who would have drowned.

For his noble, selfless act
everybody came to thank him.

"Whatever you want, you can have,"
they told Styopa, openhanded.

"I don't want a thing for me.
Nope, I saved that kid for free."

Now a train comes rumbling near—
whistle blowing, steam cascading.
At one stop, the engineer
turns back to the stoker, saying,

"I have seen my share of tracks,
lots of stations, out and back,
and I can say without a doubt,
that new signal just came out."

They approach the railway signal.
What is going on? What's that?
Why, it's not a sign at all . . .
No, it's Styopa, standing tall.

He stands unmoving and announces,
"Rains have washed the track away.
I stood and raised my hand on purpose
to let you know that trouble waits."

What's that smoke above our heads?
What's that ruckus on the street?
A house has just gone up in flames;
neighbors watch and curse the blaze.
Firefighters climb the ladder,
trying to protect the place.

High up, the attic has ignited;
pigeons pound against the window.
In the crowd, the children, hopeless,
plead aloud to Uncle Styopa,
"Can it really be—our birds,
not just our home, will also burn?"

Uncle Styopa, from the sidewalk,
reaches up into the attic.
Through the awful smoke and flames
his arm thrusts in to offer aid.

Styopa opens up the window.
From the attic out come whizzing
eighteen pigeons. In their wake,
one small sparrow soars away.

Everyone tells him they're thankful:
he saved the birds, and that's the reason
they propose that he should sign up
for the fire brigade to aid them.

But Stepan tells all the folks,
the firefighters too, "No, no!
I intend to join the navy.
Sure, I'm tall; I hope they'll take me."

In the hallway, laughs and whispers.
In the hallway, conversation.
In the office, Uncle Styopa
at a health examination.

He stands up. A nurse politely
asks him if he could bend down.
"We can't reach you! You're gigantic!"
say the doctors in frustration.

"Everything, from joints to vision,
we'll investigate for you.
Can you see into the distance?
Can you hear sounds high and low?"

They examine Uncle Styopa,
put him on the scale and gush,
"This is one well-nourished body!
Your big heart beats like a drum.

You're quite tall, but that's all right.
Our forces will take you on sight!

But you'll never drive a tank . . .
You won't fit inside the thing.
And the infantry won't do . . .
Enemies will notice you.

At your size, it would be awkward
riding in an aircraft's cockpit.
Plus, your legs would start to bug you—
you would have nowhere to put them.

There aren't horses that can stand
a guy as big as you, comrade.
But the navy needs good sailors,
so prepare to serve your nation!"

"I am ready for my service,"
Styopa's voice at once booms out.
"So, I'm headed off to sea.
Send me out, send me now!"

Winter passed, and so did summer.
Then another winter came.
"Uncle Styopa, how've you been?"
But our letters went unanswered,
not a single word came in . . .

And then one day, on the bridge
by building number 8 slash 1,
trudging in a sailor's coat,
a man of Styopa's size was seen.

Comrades, which of you can guess,
who this mighty sailor is?
As he walks,
the unswept snow
crunches underneath his boots.

He wears trousers, pressed and pleated,
and a greatcoat with a belt.
Anchors gleam on both his shoulders;
woolen gloves protect his hands.

So, the sailor has come home,
but to us he's still unknown.
Then the children start to quiz him,
"Who is it you're here to visit?"

Uncle Styopa turns around,
lifts his hand in a salute,
and then says, "I have returned.
The navy granted me shore leave.

Quite a trip. I haven't slept.
My legs aren't used to dry land yet.
Now I'll rest. And change my shirt.
Let me sit a little while.
Come and see me after teatime.
I'll tell you a hundred tales!

About the war, about the air raids,
about the battleship *Marat,*
and how I got a little wounded
fighting hard for Leningrad."

Now, the children all are proud—
Pioneers, Octobrist Scouts—
that they're friends with Uncle Styopa,
their true hero—noble, knight-like.

Sometimes when he hurries home,
the kids will shout, "Hey, how's it goin'?"
Now those kids call Uncle Styopa
by a brand-new nickname: "Lighthouse."

DANIIL KHARMS (1905–1942) continued to write poetry and prose for children until his second arrest in 1941. His short story "Why Don't We Write a Story?" was written in 1935. The poem "A Man Left His House," written in 1937, is often seen as a prescient foretelling of his own fate and that of many of his contemporaries who likewise disappeared in Stalin's Gulag. "Once There Was a Little Man" (1940), one of Kharms's last poems, was published in *Hedgehog* shortly before his arrest and death.

Why Don't We Write a Story?

Translated by Ilya Bernstein

"Why don't we write a story?" said Vanya, taking out his notebook and putting it on the table.

"All right." said Lenochka, sitting down next to him.

Vanya picked up a pencil and wrote, "Once upon a time, there was a king."

Then Vanya stopped writing and started thinking. In the meantime, Lenochka peeked into his notebook and read what he had written.

"Hold on," said Lenochka. "Everyone knows THAT story."

"What story?" asked Vanya.

"You know," said Lenochka, "the one about the king who was in the middle of eating dessert, when he suddenly choked on a cookie. So, the queen started hitting the king on the back to see if the cookie would budge. Only the king thought she was fighting, so he hit her on the head with a cup. So, the queen became furious and hit the king with a plate. So, the king hit the queen with a pot. So, the queen hit the king with a chair. So, the king jumped up and pushed over the table on top of her. But the queen crawled out from under the table and pushed over the cupboard on top of him. But the king crawled out from under the cupboard and threw his crown at the queen. But the queen grabbed the king by his beard and threw him out the window. But the king came right back through a different window and pushed the queen into the oven. But the queen crawled up through the chimney, climbed out onto the roof, shimmied down a drainpipe, and came in again through the window. Meanwhile, the king was busy trying to light the oven. The queen sneaked up behind the king—and pushed the king into the oven. And the king fell right in and got burned to a crisp. That's the whole story."

"What a silly story!" said Vanya. "I wanted to write something totally different."

"So?" said Lenochka. "Write!'"

Vanya picked up the pencil and wrote, "Once upon a time, there was an outlaw."

"Hold it!" shouted Lenochka. "I've heard that story too."

"Really?" asked Vanya.

"Sure," said Lenochka. "It's all about this outlaw who was escaping from the jail guards and jumped on a horse, but missed the saddle and came crashing down on the ground. The outlaw shook his fist at the horse and jumped up again, but again he missed the saddle and came crashing down on the ground. The outlaw got up off the ground, cursed three times in a row, and jumped up again, but missed the saddle again and came crashing down on the ground. This time the outlaw pulled out his gun, fired three shots in the air, and jumped up once more, but again missed the saddle and came crashing down on the ground. The outlaw threw his hat on the ground and jumped up and down on top it, and then jumped on the horse once again, but again he missed the saddle, came crashing down on the ground, and broke his leg. That's when the horse decided to move away from the outlaw. The outlaw ran up to the horse, limping, and WHACK!—gave it a whack on the head. Only now the horse just left. At this point, the jail guards arrived, caught the outlaw, and took him off to jail."

"All right," said Vanya. "So, I won't write about the outlaw."

"So, who ARE you going to write about?" asked Lenochka.

"I will write about a blacksmith," said Vanya.

He picked up his pencil and wrote, "Once upon a time, there was a blacksmith."

"Not so fast!" cried Lenochka. "I know that one too!"

"Well?" said Vanya, putting his pencil down on the table.

"Well," said Lenochka, "once upon a time, there was a blacksmith. And one day this blacksmith was hammering a horseshoe, when he raised his hammer so fast that the head of the hammer flew off the handle, went out the window, killed four pigeons, bounced off the water tower, broke a window in the mayor's house, went through the mayor's living room, where the mayor and his wife were playing checkers, broke another window in the mayor's house, and flew outside. Then it tore down a street sign, knocked over a policeman, and bounced off the head of Professor Shoestring, who had just stepped outside for a breath of fresh air. After bouncing off the head of Professor Shoestring, the head of the hammer started flying back in the opposite direction, knocked over the very same policeman for the second time in a row, swept a pair of scraggly cats off a roof, knocked over a cow, killed four sparrows, flew back into the smithy, and landed right back on the handle of the hammer, which the blacksmith was still holding up in the air. All of this happened so fast that the blacksmith had no idea about any of it and just kept on hammering the horseshoe as if nothing had happened."

"Fine," said Vanya. "Forget the blacksmith. I have another idea. I'm going to write a story about myself."

And Vanya picked up the pencil and wrote, "Once upon a time, there was a boy named Vanya."

"But there already IS a story about Vanya," said Lenochka. "Once upon a time, there was a boy named Vanya. One day, Vanya walked into—"

"WAIT!" cried Vanya. "I was going to write a story about MYSELF!"

"There's already one about you, too," said Lenochka.

"That can't be," said Vanya.

"Yes, it can," said Lenochka.

"Oh no, it can't," said Vanya.

"Oh yes, it can," said Lenochka. "It's called WHY DON'T WE WRITE A STORY? and it's all about you."

Lenochka went over to the bookshelf and took down a book called WHY DON'T WE WRITE A STORY? She gave it to Vanya, and Vanya read it straight through from beginning to end.

But you already know what THAT story was about, because you've just read it yourself!

A Man Left His House[4]

Translated by Matvei Yankelevich and Eugene Ostashevsky

A man once walked out of his house
with a bag and a walking stick,
and off he went,
and off he went
and he never did turn back.

He walked on straight and forward
and only looked ahead,
he never slept,
nor drank nor slept,
nor slept nor drank nor ate.

Then once upon a morning
he entered a dark wood

---

4 Reprinted with permission from *OBERIU: An Anthology of Russian Absurdism*. Edited by Eugene Ostashevsky. Evanston: Northwestern University Press, 2006, p.140.

and on that day,
and on that day
he disappeared for good.

If anywhere at all you meet
with him by any chance,
then run and tell,
then run and tell,
then run and tell us, please.

Once There Was a Little Man

Translated by Ilya Bernstein

Once there was a little man
Four pounds and a half
And this very little man
All he did was laugh!

It was always hee hee hee
Ho ho ho
And woink woink!
He just had to ha ha ha
Ho ho ho
And oink oink!

When a spider came his way
Filling him with fear
He just laughed his fear away
Pulling on his beard

Giggle giggle hee hee hee
hey hey hey
and wah wah!
He just couldn't ha ha ha
Giggle giggle
wow wow!

And encountering a fly
He was seized with wrath
But he told his wrath: goodbye!
And began to laugh

Ha ha ha and hop hop hop
giggle giggle
woy woy!
Help me boys I cannot stop
giggle giggle
oy oy!

VITALY BIANKI (1894–1959) published "The Little Ant Who Hurried Home" in 1936. Bianki stated in his diary that it took some time to compose this "insect book," and that he rewrote it three times. Bianki consulted his brother, the entomologist Lev Bianki, for advice when preparing this work. The 1983 animated film "The Journey of the Ant", which is based on Bianki's tale, was directed by Eduard Nazarov.

The Little Ant Who Hurried Home

Translated by Andrea Lanoux

Once a little Ant climbed a birch tree. He reached the top, looked down below, and saw his own little anthill off in the distance.

He sat on a leaf and thought, "I'll rest here a bit before going down."

Ants have a rule: as soon as the sun starts to set, they hurry home. And when the sun goes down, they close up the anthill—every entryway and exit—and go to sleep. If anyone is late, then they have to sleep outside.

The sun was going down over the forest. The Ant sat on his leaf and thought, "It's fine, I'll make it. It's faster going down."

The leaf had seen better days: it was yellow and dry. A wind came up and ripped it from the branch. The leaf blew through the forest, over the river, and through the village.

The little Ant was carried away on the leaf, tossed from side to side, nearly dead from fright.

The wind carried the leaf to a meadow beyond the village and dropped it there. The leaf fell on a rock, wounding the little Ant's legs.

There he lay, thinking, "How stupid of me—now I won't make it home. Flat ground, all around. If I weren't hurt, I would just run home, but that's just the problem—I've injured my legs. Woe is me!"

The Ant looked around: a Geo-Meter Caterpillar was lounging nearby. He looked like a worm, but with legs in the front and back.

"Geo-Meter, Geo-Meter," said the Ant, "Take me home. I've hurt my teeny legs."

"You won't bite me, will you?"

"Of course not."

"Well then, climb aboard. I'll take you."

The little Ant scrambled on to the Geo-Meter's back. He made an arc with his body, pulled his back legs forward, and brought his tail to his head. Suddenly, he stood up tall, as tall as his body would reach, then fell back down to the ground, straight as a stick. In this manner he surveyed the ground, measuring it with the length of his body, then pulling his body up into an arc. Thus, he went.

The little Ant was carried along, flying up to the sky and down to the ground, upside down, then up, then down.

"I can't take it!" he shouted. "Stop, or I'll bite you!"

The Geo-Meter came to a halt and stretched out along the ground. The little Ant climbed off, barely catching his breath.

He looked around and saw a meadow up ahead covered with freshly cut grass. A Daddy Longlegs was striding through the meadow, his legs like stilts and his head swaying low.

"Longlegs, hey Longlegs, please take me home! I've hurt my teeny legs."

"Well then, climb aboard. I'll take you."

The little Ant had to climb up the spider's leg to his knee, then slide back down his leg to his back, since the Daddy Longlegs's knees were higher than his back.

The Daddy Longlegs started moving his stilts, putting one leg here and another there. All eight legs flashed before the Ant's eyes like knitting needles. But the spider's pace was slow, and he dragged his body near the ground. The little Ant got tired of riding like this. He nearly bit the spider by accident. Just then, by good fortune, they came out on to a smooth path. The Daddy Longlegs stopped.

"Hop off," he said. "A Ground Beetle is coming, she is swifter than I am." The little Ant jumped down.

"Ground Beetle, dear Ground Beetle," said the Ant, "Take me home. I've hurt my teeny legs."

"Hop on, I'll take you."

As soon as the little Ant scrambled on to her back, the Ground Beetle took off! She had an even stride, like that of a horse. The six-legged horse ran like the wind, as if flying through the air with fluid movements. In a flash they had reached a potato field.

"Get off now," said the Ground Beetle. "My legs weren't made to hop over potato mounds. You'll have to find another ride."

He had to dismount. To an ant, a potato field looks like a thick forest. Even if his legs had been all right, he would have to run all day in order to cross it. And the sun was already low in the sky.

Suddenly the little Ant heard someone peep, "Hey Ant, get on my back. I'll take you."

The Ant turned around and saw a tiny Flea Beetle standing next to him, barely visible in the dirt.

"But you're so small! You won't be able to lift me."

"And you're so big! I said hop on."

The Ant somehow fit on the back of the Flea Beetle, but he barely managed to tuck in his legs.

"Are you on?"

"I guess I am."

"Then stay there."

The little Flea Beetle gathered his thick, hind legs beneath him, which looked like folding springs—then click!—he straightened them. Suddenly, he was on another mound. Click! Another mound. Click! And a third. In this way he clicked across the field to the base of a fence.

"Can you make it over?" the little Ant asked.

"The fence is too high. Ask the Grasshopper—he can do it."

So, he turned to a Grasshopper passing by:

"Grasshopper, Grasshopper, take me home. I've hurt my teeny legs."

"Hop on my neck."

The little Ant sat on his nape of his neck. The Grasshopper folded his long legs in half, straightened them with a snap, and flew high into the air like the little Flea Beetle. Then the wings on his back popped out, catapulted the Grasshopper over the fence, and gently placed him on the ground.

"Station!" said the Grasshopper. "We've arrived."

The little Ant looked out before him and saw a river. He could swim for a year and never cross it. And the sun was setting ever lower in the sky.

The Grasshopper said, "I can't cross this river. It's mighty wide. Wait here, I'll get the Water Strider. He can ferry you across."

He snapped his wings as only he can do, and lo—a little boat on legs was gliding across the water. But it wasn't a boat, it was a Water Strider.

"Water Strider, Water Strider, take me home! I've hurt my teeny legs."

"All right, hop aboard. I'll take you over."

The little Ant got on. The Water Strider hopped and strode across the water, as if on dry land. The sun was now very low in the sky.

"Faster, my friend!" implored the Ant. "They won't let me in!"

"I'll go faster then," said the Water Strider.

So, he picked up the pace. The Water Strider pushed off with his legs and skated across the water, as if on an ice rink. They reached the other shore with incredible speed.

"Can you do that on dry ground?" asked the little Ant.

"I can't do that on land, my legs can't glide. Look here: we're at the woods. Find yourself another ride."

The little Ant looked before him and saw a towering forest rising up above the river, scraping the sky. The sun had already hidden behind the trees. Oh no, the little Ant wouldn't make it home!

"Look," said the Water Strider, "here comes a ride for you."

The little Ant saw a June Bug crawling—a bumbling, lumbering beetle. A ride like that couldn't make it very far. Still, he listened to the Water Strider.

"June Bug, June Bug, carry me home! I've hurt my teeny legs."

"Where do you live?"

"In the anthill beyond the forest."

"Oh, that's far . . . Well, what can you do? Hop on, I'll get you there."

The little Ant climbed up his steep, beetley side.

"Are you on?"

"Yes."

"Where are you sitting?"

"On your back."

"Silly! Climb on to my head."

The little Ant climbed on to the June Bug's head. It's a good thing he didn't stay on his back: the beetle's back split in two, and two stiff wings rose up. They looked like two hoods on a car. Beneath them other wings appeared and unfolded: thin, transparent wings, wider and longer than the first.

The June Bug huffed and puffed, as if starting an engine: "Oof, oof, oof!"

"Faster, old man!" pleaded the little Ant. "Speed it up, dear friend!"

The June Bug didn't reply. He only huffed, "Oof, oof, oof!"

Suddenly, the thin wings fluttered and started humming—"Zzzzzzzzz! Click-click-click . . ." The June Bug soared into the air. Buoyed by the wind, he shot high above the forest like a cork.

The little Ant looked down: the sun was but a sliver on the horizon.

The June Bug rushed with such speed that it took the little Ant's breath away.

"Zzzzzzzzz! Click-click-click . . ." dashed the beetle, cutting through the air like a bullet.

The forest flashed below—then it disappeared.

Here was his familiar birch, and underneath it his anthill.

At the very top of the birch, the beetle turned off his engine and landed on a branch—plop!

"Dear old man!" entreated the little Ant, "How am I supposed to get down? I've already hurt my legs, next I'll break my neck!"

The June Bug folded his thin wings along his back. Then he put down the top, and carefully tucked his gossamer wings under the hood.

He thought for a moment, then said, "I have no idea. I won't take you to the anthill—you ants bite too hard. Get there yourself as you like."

The little Ant looked down and saw his sweet home, right there under the birch.

He glimpsed the sun—its head was skimming the top of the horizon. He looked around—just leaves and twigs, twigs and leaves. He couldn't make it now even if he were to throw himself down, headlong below!

Just then, on a neighboring leaf, he saw a Leafroller Caterpillar pulling a silk thread from her body and winding it around a twig.

"Caterpillar, Caterpillar, help me get home! I have just a second before they close up the anthill for the night!"

"Leave me alone! Can't you see I'm doing my thing, spinning my yarn?"

"Everyone else took pity on me—you're the only one who's turned me away!"

The little Ant couldn't stop himself: he lunged at her and bit her!

The Caterpillar pulled her legs in from fright, then somersaulted below.

The little Ant was hanging on to her tightly. The trip didn't last long: something caught them from above. The two swayed back and forth on a silk thread that had gotten caught on a twig.

The Ant swayed back and forth attached to the Leafroller, as on a swing. The thread grew longer and longer extending from the Leafroller's belly, stretching but not breaking. Down, down, down went the little Ant and the Leafroller.

Below the ants were rushing around, closing up the anthill for the night. They closed all of the openings except one. The little Ant hopped off the Leafroller Caterpillar and sped inside.

Then down went the sun.

ALEKSEY TOLSTOY (1883–1945) was born in Nikolaevsk in the Samara region. He began his career as a poet, before going on to publish many renowned books of prose, including novels, fairy tales, and short stories. He also wrote several plays. After the Bolshevik Revolution, Tolstoy left Russia and settled in Berlin. In 1922, he published the autobiographical work *Nikita's Childhood.* Tolstoy came from a noble family, but he accepted the new regime and returned to the Soviet Union where he published two novels of science fiction, *Aelita* (1923) and *The Hyperboloid of Engineer Garin* (1927). He authored a two-volume work of historical fiction, *Peter the Great* (1934), and the trilogy *The Road to Calvary* (1922–1941). Tolstoy received three Stalin Prizes over the course of his career. His children's book *The Golden Key, or the Adventures of Buratino* (1936) is an adaptation of Carlo Collodi's *Pinocchio*; in Tolstoy's version, however, the hero never becomes a real boy. The excerpts below from *The Adventures of Buratino* include three chapters. The illustration to the 1948 edition is by **Aminadav Kanevsky** (1898–1976), the book's second illustrator (after Bronislav Malakhovsky).

Aleksey Tolstoy, *The Golden Key, or the Adventures of Buratino*, illus. Aminadav Kanevsky (Moscow: Gosudarstvennoe izdatel'stvo detskoi literatury, 1948). Courtesy of Columbia University Libraries.

The Golden Key, or the Adventures of Buratino **[excerpts]**

Translated by Jane Bugaeva

Carlo Makes a Wooden Doll and Names It Buratino

Carlo lived in a cupboard under the stairs where he had nothing but a beautiful hearth on the wall across from the door. But the beautiful hearth, the fire inside it, and the small kettle boiling in the flames weren't real—they were painted on a piece of old canvas. Carlo walked into his cupboard, sat on the only chair by a table missing a leg, picked up a log, twirling it this way and that, and began carving a doll out of it.

"What should I name it?" he wondered. "I know—I'll call it Buratino. This name will bring me luck. I knew one family, everyone in it was named Buratino—the mother, the father, the children: all Buratino. They lived a happy, worry-free life."

First, he carved hair into the log, then a forehead, then eyes—when suddenly the eyes opened and stared straight at him. Carlo didn't show his fright and only asked gently, "Little wooden eyes, why are you looking at me like that?" But the doll was silent—probably because it didn't yet have a mouth.

Carlo whittled the cheeks and then an ordinary nose—but all of a sudden the nose began to stretch and grow all on its own, becoming so long and pointy that Carlo yelled out, "No, too long . . ." He went to trim the tip—but no such luck! The nose twisted and turned away from his knife and remained long and pointy—a very curious nose.

Carlo began working on the mouth. As soon as he'd carved the lips, the mouth opened and laughed, "He he he, ha ha ha!" and a narrow red tongue stuck out of it, teasing him. Carlo no longer paid these antics any mind and continued whittling, cutting, and carving. He made the doll a chin, a neck, shoulders, a body, and arms. He'd barely finished carving the last finger when Buratino began hammering Carlo's bald spot with his little fists and tickling and pinching him.

"Listen up," said Carlo. "I haven't even finished making you and you're already causing trouble. What's next? Huh?" And he looked at Buratino sternly. And Buratino looked back at his Papa Carlo with his round, mouse-like eyes.

Carlo used slivers of kindling to make long legs with big feet. When he'd finished, he set the wooden boy on the floor to teach him how to walk. Buratino wobbled on his thin legs, took one step, then another, then a skip, a hop, right to the door and out onto the street!

Carlo, worried, ran after him, "Hey troublemaker, get back here!"

No chance! Buratino ran down the street quick as a bunny, his wooden soles tap-tapping, tap-tapping against the cobblestones.

"Grab him!" yelled Carlo. People on the street laughed, pointing at the running Buratino. At the intersection stood a huge police officer with a curled mustache and a triangular cap. He saw the running wooden boy and stood with his legs spread wide, blocking the whole street. Buratino tried to slip between his legs, but the officer grabbed him by the nose and held him like that until Papa Carlo caught up.

"Just you wait, I'll deal with you . . ." panted Carlo. He went to put Buratino in his coat pocket, but Buratino didn't want to spend this cheery day stuck upside down in a pocket for all to see—he easily wriggled himself free, flopped onto the street, and played dead.

"Oh dear," said the officer. "That's not good."

Pedestrians began to gather, looking at Buratino and shaking their heads.

"The poor lad, he must have starved," said some.

"Carlo must've beaten him to death," said others. "That old organ-grinder is only pretending to be a good man, he's bad, he's evil."

Hearing all this, the officer grabbed poor Carlo by his collar and dragged him to the police station. Carlo's shoes stirred up dust and he moaned loudly, "Oh, why'd I ever make that wooden boy?"

When the street emptied, Buratino lifted his head, looked all around, and quickly ran home.

Buratino Sells His Textbook and Buys a Ticket to the Puppet Show

Early one morning Buratino put his textbook in his bag and ran off to school. On his way, he didn't even look at the sweets on display in shop windows: poppyseed triangles dipped in honey, sweet buns, and lollipops in the shape of roosters. He didn't look at the little boys flying kites. The striped cat Basilio was crossing the street, and Buratino could've grabbed him by the tail—but he resisted even this temptation.

As Buratino got closer to school, the sound of cheerful music grew louder and louder. It was coming from the nearby shores of the Mediterranean Sea.

"Tootle-too," trilled a flute.

"Zin zin zin," quivered a violin.

"Clang clang," rang the cymbals.

"Boom!" banged a drum.

School was to his right, the music was coming from his left. Buratino began stumbling—his legs, of their own accord, turned towards the shore, where he heard:

"Tootle-tootle-too."

"Clang-zin-zin, clang-zin-zin."

"Boom!"

"School's not going anywhere, is it?" said Buratino to himself. "I'll just peek in and listen, then head right to school." And he took off towards the shore. He saw a canvas tent adorned with colorful flags, flapping in the sea breeze. Four musicians played atop the tent, dancing along to their own music. Down below, a plump, smiling woman sold tickets. A big crowd gathered at the entrance: boys and girls, soldiers, lemonade vendors, wet-nurses with babies, firefighters, mail carriers. Everyone was reading a big sign:

PUPPET SHOW
ONE
SHOW
ONLY!
HURRY!
HURRY!
HURRY!

Buratino tugged on a boy's sleeve, "Excuse me, how much is a ticket?"

"Four soldo, wooden boy," said the boy.

"You see, little boy, I forgot my coin purse at home . . . would you lend me four soldo?"

The boy gave a snide whistle. "Do I look like a fool?"

"I reeeally want to see the puppet show!" said Buratino tearfully. "I'll sell you my beautiful jacket for four soldo."

"That paper jacket for four soldo? No way."

"How about my nice cap?"

"That little thing is only good for catching tadpoles. No way."

Buratino wanted to see the puppet show so bad that his nose grew cold. "In that case I'll sell you my brand-new textbook."

"Does it have pictures?"

"Beauuutiful pictures and big letters."

"Alright, I'll take it." The boy took the book and reluctantly counted out four soldo. Buratino ran up to the plump, smiling woman and squeaked, "I'll take a seat in the front row for the one and only puppet show!"

On His Way Home Buratino Runs into Two Swindlers—Basilio the Cat and Alice the Fox

One morning Buratino was counting his money—he had as many gold coins as fingers on his hand: five. He clutched the gold in his hand and skipped home, singing along the way, "I'm going to buy Papa Carlo a new coat, I'm going to buy lots of poppyseed triangles and rooster lollipops."

When the puppet-show tent and its fluttering flags disappeared from view, he saw two swindlers gloomily ambling down the dusty road: Alice the fox, hobbling on three legs, and blind Basilio the cat. (It wasn't the cat Buratino had seen yesterday on the street, though this cat was also striped and was also named Basilio.)

Buratino wanted to walk right past them, but Alice called sweetly, "Hello, kind Buratino! Where are you hurrying off to?"

"Home. To Papa Carlo."

Alice sighed and continued ever so sweetly, "Oh, I don't know if you'll catch poor Carlo alive . . . he's not well from hunger and cold . . ."

"Haven't you heard I'm rich?" Buratino opened his hand, showing his five gold coins. The fox involuntarily reached her paw towards the money, while the cat's blind eyes suddenly opened wide, glistening like two green lanterns. But Buratino didn't notice any of it.

"Kind, darling Buratino, what are you going to do with that money?"

"I'll buy a coat for Papa Carlo. I'll buy a new textbook."

"A textbook? Oh, ho!" said Alice, shaking her head. "Nothing good will come from studying. Look at me, I studied and studied . . . and now I'm walking around on three legs!"

"A textbook!" growled Basilio and snorted into his whiskers. "That's how I lost my eyesight—from all that cursed studying!"

An elderly raven sat on a dry branch near the road, listening in.

"Lies! Lies!" she cawed. In an instant, Basilio jumped up and swatted the raven off the branch, tearing out half her tail feathers—she barely got away. Then the cat went back to pretending to be blind.

"Why'd you do that to the raven, Basilio?" asked Buratino.

"I'm blind, you know, I thought it was a dog on that branch."

The three of them continued along the dusty road.

"Smart, sensible Buratino, would you like to have ten times as much money?" asked Alice.

"Of course, I would! But how?"

"Easy. Just come with us."

"Where to?"

"To the Land of Fools."

Buratino thought for a moment. "No thanks, I think I'll just go home."

"Please . . . we aren't pulling your leg," said Alice. "It'll be your loss."

"Your loss," growled Basilio.

"You're standing in your own way," said Alice.

"You're standing in your own way," growled Basilio. "You could turn your five coins into a pile of gold!"

Buratino stopped and opened his mouth, "No way!"

The fox sat on her tail, licking her lips. "Let me explain. In the Land of Fools there is a magical place called the Field of Miracles. In the field, you dig a hole, say three times: 'krex, fex, pex,' put a coin in the hole, cover it with soil, sprinkle some salt on top, water it generously, and go to sleep. In the morning a small sapling will grow there, but instead of leaves it will be laden with golden coins. Got it?"

Buratino jumped up, "No way!"

"Let's go, Basilio," said Alice, turning up her nose in a huff. "He doesn't believe us. Too bad . . ."

"No no," yelled Buratino. "I believe you, I believe you! Quick, take me to the Land of Fools!"

ALEXANDER VVEDENSKY (1904–941) wrote "Lullaby" in 1937 when his son Peter was born. It was first published in the children's magazine *Cricket.*

Lullaby

Translated by Eugene Ostashevsky

I will now begin to count:
One, two, three, and four, and five.
When I reach the number five,
Everybody fall asleep!

Sleep, it walks around the roads,
One, two, three, and four, and *piat'.*
Orders everyone around:
Sleep. Sleep. Sleep. *Spat'.*

Sleep, it walks along the street.
There it sees a Pussycat
Walking on almost five feet.
Sleep says, Pussy, fall asleep!
One, two, three, *chetyre, piat'.*
Sleep. Sleep. *Spat'. Spat'.*

Who is still awake? The Dolls.
As Sleep walks into their room
The Dolls let their eyelids close,
Teddy Bear falls asleep.
One, two, *tri, chetyre, piat'.*
Sleep. *Spat'. Spat'. Spat'.*

Sleep, it walks up to your bed,
And it yawns and whispers still:
Trees and Bushes have retired,
Fall asleep, my tired Child.
One, *dva, tri, chetyre, piat'.*
Spat'. Spat'. Spat'. Spat'.

I will count once again:
Raz, dva, tri, chetyre, piat'.
Spat'.

AGNIA BARTO (1901–1981), born into a Moscow Jewish family, became a children's poet on the advice of Anatoly Lunacharsky, the first Soviet minister of education. Barto wrote short, easy to memorize poems for small children. Their ordinary heroes with unremarkable names—Tamara, Lyuba, Tanya, Volodya—were familiar and relatable to young readers. From 1965 to 1973, Barto anchored the radio program *Find a Person,* which helped people locate family members lost during World War II. Over the course of those nine years, Barto helped reunite more than a thousand families. In 1968, she authored a book by the same title. Barto also wrote several movie scripts, including the famous comedy *Foundling* (1940). Her poems for young readers were published and republished regularly, and they were the first texts many Soviet children learned by heart and recited. In 1968, an asteroid was named after Barto, signaling her cultural significance. The poem "The House That Moved" was published in 1938 with illustrations by **Konstantin Rotov** (1902–1959), describing the relocation of a house on Serafimovich Street in Moscow. "They Left" was included in the 1940 collection *Poems.* "Off to School" was written and first published in the 1940s.

Agnia Barto, *The House That Moved,* illus. Konstantin Rotov (Moscow: Melik-Pashaev, 2011). Courtesy of the Russian State Children's Library.

The House That Moved

Translated by Anna Krushelnitskaya

By the Moscow River Bridge,
The river flows with all its might.
By the Moscow River Bridge,
One street became a little tight.

Every day, the traffic's thicker.
Every day, the drivers bicker.
The policemen sigh and say,
"This corner house is in the way!"

A boy named Mitya, he had gone
To summer camp for summer fun.
Now, after many weeks away,
He's on the Moscow train today.

Off the train, and he goes straight
To his house—No house! No gate!
Mitya blinks and rubs his eyes
In a flabbergasted state.

His house used to be
Right here!
How could it simply
Disappear?

"Where's my Building Number 4?
It stood here big and tall before!"
Mitya cries to a policeman.
"I can't find it anymore!

I came home from the Black Sea.
Home is where I need to be!
That big building shouldn't hide—
I have left my mom inside!"

The policeman said to Mitya:
"Your big house was sticking out,
So, we dragged it round the corner
To create a better route.

Take this lane, if you don't mind.
Your house should not be hard to find."

Mitya whispered, nearly weeping:
"That just sounds like crazy talk.

Am I dreaming? Am I sleeping?
Did you tell me houses walk?"

Mitya went off running, calling
To his neighbors, and they said:
"Yes, dear boy, we have been rolling.
Days go by—we roll ahead.

These old walls are softly gliding.
These old mirrors hardly shake.
In the cupboard, cups are riding.
Not a single lamp did break."

"You moved the house,
But you don't leave it?!"
Mitya couldn't quite
Believe it!

"I could ride my house in summer,
Take it to the country, somewhere.
Then, my neighbors will stop by
To wave my leaving home goodbye!

We won't have to do our homework!
Tell the teachers, if you like:
'All my textbooks are at home,
But then my home—it took a hike!'

We go for firewood down the hollow—
After us, our house will trot.
We go play—our house will follow.
We are home—our house is . . . not.

'Your house has gone to Leningrad
To attend a big parade.
It should be back at dawn tomorrow.
Hopefully, it's not delayed.'

The house will say to every renter,
'Read the sign before you enter:

Closed for business! Off to sea!
Please stop running after me.'

That's no good!" the boy decided.
"We own homes; they must obey.
Houses shouldn't run unguided.
People have the final say.

We go floating where we want,
Through deep blue sky or deep blue sea!
We move houses, if we want,
To where *we* think
They need to be."

They Left

Translated by Anna Krushelnitskaya

They gave the pup milk, so he grows
A strong and healthy pet.
At night, they sneak on tippy-toes
Across the house to feel his nose,
To see if it is wet.

They taught the pup to sit and stay,
They gave him sticks for toys.
Although he whines about his leash,
He skips behind the boys.

He gives all strangers little growls
With a big dog's brawn.
But then, his boys got in a truck
And—just like that—were gone.

He waited up: When can we play?
Maybe, when evening falls?
His dog life always went this way:

With big bright bonfires every day,
With morning bugle calls.

He barked at dark and scary trees
Until he'd almost wheeze.

Alone, he lay to sigh and sag.
All he could do was brood.
His lonely tail just wouldn't wag.
He lay there like an empty bag.
He wouldn't touch his food.

By then the boys had turned around
Midway, to pick him up.
He almost knocked them to the ground,
A small, excited pup!

He leapt up from his brooding place.
He licked and nuzzled every face.
When kids were cuddling their pet—
His barks were best and loudest yet!

Off to School

Translated by Anna Krushelnitskaya

Petya couldn't stay asleep.
"What was the matter?" you might say.
It's the first day of his First Grade!
He is starting school today.

He is not just any kid,
Not some little squirt.
He's in first grade! He's the new kid,
With the big-kid collared shirt.

He woke up at three a.m.,
The darkest dark, the dead of night.

He thought school began without him!
He jumped out of bed in fright.

He got dressed in minutes flat,
Then grabbed his pens and off he tore!
Father, running after Petya,
Barely caught him at the door.

Next door neighbors woke right up,
Got out of bed, turned on the light;
Next door neighbors woke right up,
Went back to bed, since it was night.

He just couldn't stay in bed.
He woke up the whole house, too!
Even Grandma had a dream
That she had homework overdue.

Even Grandpa had a nightmare,
As he napped a fitful nap:
He was asked where Moscow was,
But couldn't find it on the map!

Petya couldn't stay asleep.
"What was the matter?" you might say.
It's the first day of his First Grade!
He is starting school today.

PART 3

Ordinary Children, Extraordinary Lives (1954–1988)

BORIS ZAKHODER (1918–2000) was born in Bessarabia to a Jewish family. A writer, poet, and translator of children's literature, Zakhoder volunteered for military service during both the 1939 Russo-Finnish War and World War II. In 1946, he returned to his studies at the Maxim Gorky Literary Institute in Moscow. His children's poetry has been published regularly since the 1950s. In addition to writing original poetry, he has translated Karel Čapek, Julian Tuwim, and such British classics as *Winnie-the-Pooh* by A. A. Milne, *Mary Poppins* by P. L. Travers, *Peter Pan* by J. M. Barrie, and *Alice's Adventures in Wonderland* by Lewis Carroll. In 1999, Zakhoder received the Russian Federation State Prize for lifetime contributions to children's literature. "Kitty's Sorrow" (1955), "Hedgehog" (1955), "Cooks" (1957), "No One" (1960), and "The Termite's Diet" (1965) were first published in the journals and newspapers *Youth, Pioneer Truth, Murzilka, Youth Guard,* and *Literary Russia,* and later anthologized. **Lev Tokmakov** (1928–2010) illustrated many of Zakhoder's poems.

Boris Zakhoder, *The School for Baby Birds*, illus. Lev Tokmakov (Moscow: Detskaya literatura, 1970). Courtesy of the Russian State Children's Library.

Kitty's Sorrow

Translated by Ainsley Morse

Kitty's weeping in the hall.
She's overcome
With anguish:

Awful people
Keep poor Kitty
From
Stealing
All the fish!

Hedgehog

Translated by Ainsley Morse

"Hey HEDGEHOG, why so many spikes?"
"Well, it's not that I'm warlike;
But my neighbors, as you're aware,
Are wolves and foxes, even bears!"

Cooks

Translated by Ainsley Morse

Making dinner is so easy!
It is really just a breeze,
What could be simpler, I don't know:
You just make it, and there you go!
(If Mama is making dinner.)
But sometimes Mama is not at home,
And we have to make it all on our own,
And then
(Who knows why, I'm just a beginner!)
It's very
Tricky
Making
Dinner!

No One

Translated by Ainsley Morse

We've got a scalawag at home.
The family is closing ranks.
The whole apartment's in a funk
Because of his obnoxious pranks!
It's true that no one knows his name,
But one thing's known by everyone:
The one to blame for everything
Is always only him—NO ONE!
Who was it, say, who found the sweets
In the old oaken cabinet
And threw the wrappers on the floor
Without the faintest of regrets?
Who drew pictures on the walls?
Who tore his coat up just for fun?
Who rummaged round in Papa's desk?
NO ONE, NO ONE, NO ONE!
"NO ONE is a menacing rascal!"
Said mother, her lips pressed thin.
"We cannot tolerate this mess;
It's time we punish him!
NO ONE will be allowed today
To watch TV or go play ball!"
You're laughing?
Well, my sis and I
Don't find it funny, not at all!

The Termite's Diet

Translated by Olga Bukhina

"What I eat,"
Said the termite,
"Is all perfect
And all right.

The order of each meal for me
Follows the ABCs.

Airplane,
Automobile,
Bunker, Band-aids,
And Cornmeal.
Confiture, Cardboard,
Caboose,
Dice, Diode,
Electric Fuse.
Film, Focaccia,
Football,
Fifteen Forks,
I ate them all.

Gorged on Gondola and Gauze,
Even though they gave me pause.

Chewed on Hangers,
Ate Harpoon,
Ice pick, Jacket,
Kite and Loon,

Lamp and Lectern,
Leash, Museum.
Tried Mailbox
And a Mausoleum.

Crunched on Nickel and on Nut,
Oyster, Painting, and Peanut.

Went through Q-tips
With high speed,
Very difficult, indeed.

Could not finish Rails and Razor,
Swallowed Robot,
Skirt and Taser,

Tie, Umbrella, UFO,
(Ate it all, despite the glow),

Ukulele, Vans, a few.
Wood of Walnut,
Wood of Yew,

Yacht and Xerox,
Xylophone,
Liked to chew it
To the bone,

Xiaosaurus dinosaur,
Zeppelin,
And wanted more.

I ate and ate, all this stuff,
Still, I never got enough."

His friend, also a termite,
Disagreed
And spat in spite:
"Why this diet? Why this rule?
Better to eat
Whatever's cool."

VENIAMIN KAVERIN (1902–1989) was born in Pskov. He began as a writer of short fantasy stories. In 1923, he graduated from the Leningrad Institute of Oriental Studies where he studied Arabic. In the 1920s he was a member of The Serapion Brothers literary group. Kaverin's most famous adventure novel, *The Two Captains,* was written between 1938 and 1944 and received the Stalin Prize in 1946. The novel was adapted into three films and a musical, *Nord-Ost* (2001). Kaverin's second major novel, *The Open Book* (1948–1956), portrays the lives of members of the Soviet intelligentsia. Kaverin wrote several tales for children, the first collection of which, *Three Tales,* was published in 1960 and republished as *Three Tales and One More* in 1963 with illustrations by **Valery Alfeevsky** (1906–1989). These stories range from political satire on fascism, and arguably also Stalinism, in "The Tale of Mitya and Masha, the Happy Chimney-Sweeper and Master Golden Hands" (1938), to the lyricism of everyday life in "The Sandglass" and "Many Good People and One Envious One."

Veniamin Kaverin, *Three Tales and One More*, illus. Valery Alfeevsky (Moscow: Detgiz, 1963).

Many Good People and One Envious One [excerpts]

Translated by Katherine E. Young

Tanya Sets Out for the Blue Globe Pharmacy

The typist of the Green Woodlands Bureau stood at the window, and suddenly—ding!—a golden ring broke the glass and rolled under the bed with a clink. It was the ring she'd lost—or thought she'd lost—twenty years before on her wedding day.

The dentist of the Puppet Theater was thirsty that night. He got up and, in the carafe of water, discovered all the gold teeth that had ever gone missing from his office.

The director of the Bathrobe Store returned from vacation and found the gold eyeglasses that had been stolen from him before he became the director of the Bathrobe Store. They lay gleaming in their former place on his desk, between the ashtray and the letter opener.

For a good two days the whole city talked about nothing but these mysteries. On every corner you could hear people discussing the subject:

"A silver cupholder?"

"Ah, does that mean they're returning not just gold but silver things, too?"

"Seems like it! And even copper things, if they were shined up with tooth powder."

"Amazing!"

"Just imagine! And in the same little box from which they disappeared!"

"Fiddlesticks! People don't voluntarily return precious things."

"Well, who, then?"

"Birds. Professor Penochkin states that it's birds specifically, and moreover not jackdaws, as Professor Mamlyugin suggests, but magpies, or what they call 'thieving magpies.'"

This story begins on the night when Tanya Zabotkina squatted down next to the door and listened to Mama and Dr. Myachik talk. Her father had a bad heart—she'd known that before. But she hadn't known that only a miracle could save him. That's what the Head Municipal Doctor said, and it was impossible to doubt him because he was the Head Municipal Doctor, and he never made mistakes—at least, that's what his patients insisted.

"Anyway," said Dr. Myachik, "if I were you, I'd try to stop by the Blue Globe Pharmacy."

The doctor was very old and had big green eyeglasses; there was a wart on his fat nose, and he stroked it, saying: "Sorry, it's a bad habit."

"Ah, Petr Stepanych!" answered Mama in despair.

"Suit yourself. In any case, I'll leave the prescription. The pharmacy is on Fifth Medvezhye Gory Street."

And he left, having sadly stroked his wart in the hallway mirror.

Papa had long ago fallen asleep, and Mama fell asleep, but Tanya kept thinking and thinking: "What's so special about the Blue Globe Pharmacy?"

And when the household grew quiet and you could even hear how the cat sighed and scratched behind her ear, Tanya picked up the prescription and headed for the Blue Globe Pharmacy.

It was the first time in her life that she'd walked along city streets at night. It wasn't very dark in the streets, just kind of dark. It was necessary to cross the whole city—now *that* was scary, or kind of scary. It had always seemed to Tanya that even the most difficult thing wouldn't be so difficult if you called it "kind of" difficult.

At last she came to Fifth Medvezhye Gory Street. It had just stopped raining, and the entryways glistened, exactly as if someone had drawn them in ink on glossy black paper. One of them, its door wide open, seemed to be saying: "Come on in, please, and then we'll see what's what." And right above that entrance, big blue globes burned in the windows. "Welcome" was written on one of them, and "To Our Pharmacy" was written on the other.

A small, long-nosed, gray-haired man in a well-worn green jacket stood behind the counter.

"The pharmacist," thought Tanya.

"No, the Physician-Pharmacist," responded the man, aloud.

"I beg your pardon! May I order this medicine from you?"

"No, you can't."

"Why?"

"Because the Senior Advisor for Herbal Medicines is in charge of miracles until the first of June. If he permits it, I'll prepare this medicine."

He left, and Tanya stood there alone.

What a pharmacy it was! Bottles stood on the shelves—big ones, small ones, and very tiny ones into which you could hardly fit a single tear. Porcelain squirrels hid between the bottles, crouching on their hind legs. The squirrels themselves were bottles, used for the rarest of medicines. On the frosted glass along the counter, a sign reading "Anti-Villainite" blinked on and off. While Tanya was considering what that strange word might mean, the door opened, and a chubby boy came into the pharmacy, looking timidly about him. This was Petya, the very same Petya she'd met at Young Pioneer camp a year before. But the thing was, Petya didn't look like himself. The collar of his jacket was turned up, and his cap was pulled down over his ears.

"Hello, Petya! Thank goodness we've run into each other! Now it won't be so scary going back home."

"If you're scared," Petya returned, "you can buy a pill for cowardice. But I don't need one, because I'm not afraid of anything. Besides, I'm absolutely not Petya."

Of course, it was Petya! Of course, he'd come to buy pills for cowardice. But he was ashamed when he saw Tanya, and he pretended he wasn't Petya at all.

"Ah, you're a stupid little boy," Tanya began to say, but at that moment the Physician-Pharmacist returned.

"The Advisor doesn't permit it," he said from the doorway. "He's in a terrible mood today."

"Give me back my prescription, please," begged Tanya. "Where does he live? The Head Municipal Doctor said that only a miracle could save my father."

"Hush, for heaven's sake!" said the Physician-Pharmacist, wincing painfully. "I've got a bad heart; I'm sorry for you, but this is really bad for my health. Ultimately, we've each got to take care of ourselves first. Take your prescription. He lives at Number 3 Kozikhinskaya Street."

Tanya Meets Awkward Lora and Receives a Little Box Decorated with a Drawing of a Bird

The building was an ordinary one—long, unpainted, plain. Wrapped up in a shawl full of holes, the elevator lady sat by the entrance. She looked like Baba-Yaga. She wasn't Baba-Yaga, of course, but the most ordinary old woman wrapped in a shawl full of holes.

"Ninth floor," she said grumpily.

Tanya didn't have time to collect herself before the elevator lifted off and swung open in front of a door labeled "Senior Advisor." Tanya rang the doorbell, and a child's voice asked:

"Who's there?"

"Pardon me, please, may I see . . ."

The door swung open. In the hallway stood a plump little girl who was a very pale, whitish color.

"Do you really want to see him?"

"Of course."

"Please don't be surprised that I'm asking. It's just that I never believe anybody. My father says you shouldn't trust anyone, and even if that's so, I still have to trust my own father. By the way, tell me, please, do you eat dinner twice a day?"

"No."

"I do," said the little girl with a sigh. "You see, my father worries about my health. 'Eat, eat!' And he just laughs if I say that it's plain wrong when a little girl lacks even a hint of a waist. Come, I'll show you the way. What's your name?"

"Tanya."

"Don't tell him I was complaining."

"Of course not!" [. . .]

He was a tall man, spare, black-eyed, about forty years old. His eyes were restless, and his left nostril flared unpleasantly from time to time. But everyone knows that even very good people have bad habits. Take good Dr. Myachik, who stroked the wart on his fat, kind nose all the time. And on the bright side, the Senior Advisor was smiling. Yes, yes! And you could even have called that smile good-natured, even exceptionally good-natured, if he hadn't been rubbing his long, white hands or drawing his little black head back into his shoulders.

"What do I see?" said he when the little girl came into his office. "My daughter isn't asleep yet? And you've even brought me your friend?"

"Don't make things up, Papa! You know very well that I don't have any friends. This little girl came to you on business. Her name is Tanya."

"Hello! I'm sorry to disturb you. I was sent to you by the manager at the Blue Globe Pharmacy. Please give him permission to prepare this medicine."

Why did the Senior Advisor's eyes gleam? Why did he purse his lips in such a scary way?

"Good God!" he shouted. "Your father is ill. How terrible!"

"Do you know him?"

"Of course, I do! I know him very well. Many years ago, we lived next door to each other, in the same courtyard. Every day we went swimming, and we especially loved diving. Do you suppose he remembers me? Not likely."

"He probably remembers," said Tanya politely. "By the way, he's a very good diver, even now."

"Is that so?" The Senior Advisor clutched at his heart. "Lorochka, sweetheart, please run me a cool bath. I think I'm not going to be able to fall asleep tonight, either."

You might have thought that Lora didn't want to leave the room, although there was nothing special in the fact that her father had asked her to prepare a cool bath.

"Wait for me, okay?" she whispered to Tanya and left.

"Tell me, Tanya, did Dr. Myachik warn you that that you must take the medicine first, and that your father should take it only after you do?"

"Me?"

"Yes. But if you don't want to, I'm not going to insist on it, no! You don't have to order the medicine. It's right here in the drawer."

And he held out a little box decorated with a drawing of a bird to Tanya.

"Thank you."

Tanya took the little box, nodded at him, and left. In the corridor, she opened it. Inside lay the simplest, cutest little pill. She put it in her mouth and swallowed.

What happened next is unclear—whether she turned immediately into a magpie, or whether she heard Lora just before doing so. Lora had run out of the bathroom and was shouting in horror:

"Don't swallow it!"

Petya Takes a Pill for Cowardice and Becomes Brave

What did Petya do when Tanya left the Blue Globe Pharmacy? He bought the antidote for cowardice as quickly as possible and ran after her. He was ashamed that the little girl had asked him to accompany her and he, a man, had rudely refused.

It was dark on Kozikhinskaya Street, and the neighborhood was unfamiliar. He didn't catch up to Tanya because he kept stopping with each step and clutching at the pills in his pocket.

Building Number 3 glittered ominously in the moonlight. A skinny cat with the face of a bandit sat on the curbstone. The elevator lady peering out from the entrance looked like Baba-Yaga. And some kind of bird flew out of a window and began circling around him, so low that it almost hit him with its long, forked tail. It was too much for Petya. With shaking hands, he pulled the pills from his pocket and swallowed first one and then a second one, just in case. And just like that, everything around him changed in an instant! Building Number 3 seemed to him to be the most ordinary building with peeling paint. "Scat!" he said to the cat. And he simply waved away the bird and even shook his fist at it.

He didn't know, of course, that the bird wanted to shout: "Help me, I'm Tanya!" Alas, now she could only chirp like a magpie!

"Well, Granny, how's it going?" he said to the elevator lady.

"What's your hurry?" said the elevator lady. "Sit and chat a while."

It's possible that if Petya had taken only one pill, he might have waited for Tanya by the entryway. But as you know, he had taken two, and two is definitely not the same as one.

"I've got no time to chat with you, Granny," he answered the elevator lady. "Come on, now, crank up this machine!" And in an instant, he'd lifted off for the ninth floor. "Just what I need!" he said, having looked at the copper plate, and he started to bang on the door with his hands and feet.

All people get angry when they're awakened, but especially those who have trouble falling asleep. And the Senior Advisor was angry. But the angrier he got, the politer he became. That was just his nature—a dangerous nature, his colleagues believed. He went towards Petya, smiling kindly. You might even have thought that he'd been waiting a long time for that chubby little boy to wake him up by violently thumping on the door.

"What's going on, my fine fellow?"

"What's up, Pops?" said Petya cheekily. "A little girl came to see you, tell her I'm here for her."

The Advisor looked at him thoughtfully.

"Come on in, my fine fellow," he said kindly and led Petya into his office. "Hi, Papa," he said to the Old Thrush who sat ruffling his feathers in a large, gilded cage.

"*Shnerr shtiks trenk bliks*," answered the Thrush irritably.

There were lots of books in the room: twenty-four sets of the collected works of the most famous writers, Russian and foreign. The books stood on the shelves in beautiful bindings, and they had a reproachful look—because books get angry when they aren't read.

"Do you like to read, my fine fellow?"

Of course, Petya loved to read. And not just to read, but also to recount the stories. The Senior Advisor was in luck—he'd been searching a long time for a person who could read all twenty-four sets of collected works and briefly recount their contents for him. He settled Petya in a comfortable armchair and pushed a copy of *The Three Musketeers* into his hands. Petya read the first page, then the second, and then he forgot about everything else in the world. [. . .]

The Great Envier

Long before either Petya or Tanya came into the world, there were other boys and girls, good and bad. Two boys lived in the same courtyard. One had a smooth, black little head that he loved to draw back into his shoulders, and the other was fair-haired, with a cowlick at the back of his head. Every day they swam in the river. And as they swam, they dove. That's why the Senior Advisor had asked Tanya if her father remembered how they'd loved to dive.

Once they made a bet about who could stay underwater longer. They took a deep breath and then headed to the bottom together. "One, two, three," they counted, "four, five, six." Their hearts beat more and more slowly. "Seven, eight, nine." They couldn't take any more. Whew! And they came back up to the surface. The first one up turned out to be the smooth, black little head, and only then came the fair head with a wet cowlick at the back. The black-haired boy had lost the bet.

Then they grew up, and everything that one boy liked, the other didn't. The boy with the fair hair loved to tramp around the mountains. He finally climbed so high that the eagles sent him a gold medal. But the boy with the black hair turned pale with fear just going down the stairs.

The first boy never thought of himself. He thought about those he loved, and it seemed to him that this was very simple to do. But the second boy thought only of himself. Sometimes he even wanted to try out what it would be like to think about other people, if only for a day, if only for an hour. But no matter how he worked himself up, nothing ever came of it.

Then the fair-haired boy became an artist, and it turned out that he could work miracles. At least, that's what people who'd seen his paintings said. The black-haired boy also learned to work miracles, for example, to turn people into birds and animals. But who needed those kinds of miracles? At night he thought gloomily: "Who needs my miracles?" He wore himself out with longing—all envious people wear themselves out and are full of longing.

He wrung his hands when he saw anglers sitting calmly by the water with their fishing rods. He became nauseous when he looked at young boys and girls who splashed like swallows into the water, arms outstretched. He envied anyone who was younger than he was. He didn't have any friends, and he didn't love anyone except his daughter. His father had once been Minister of the Court and Stables, and the father could never reconcile himself to having lost that title. For forty years, he didn't set foot outside his building. The father grumbled constantly, and in order to get just a little rest from him, the Great

Envier from time to time turned his father into the Old Thrush and shut him inside the gilded cage.

"What's up, Papa?" he would say, and the Thrush would answer: "*Shnerr shtiks trenk bliks.*"

You can't say that the Great Envier wasn't treated for envy—every Sunday the Physician-Pharmacist brought him drops. But they didn't help!

Sometimes he feared that his envy would pass—because, besides envy, he had only boredom in his soul, and it's easy to die of boredom. Sometimes he set about consoling himself: "You wanted to become great—and you became great," he told himself. "No one envies more than you do. You are the Great Envier. You are the Great Non-Wisher of Good." But the more he thought about himself, the more he remembered that clear summer day when two boys sat underwater and counted: "One, two, three"—that day when he lost the bet and envy first awoke in his heart.

AGNIA BARTO (1901–1981) published "Bedtime" in 1963 in a collection of the same title. This pensive poem describes a child's emotions and longing for connection, themes echoed in Masha Rupasova's 2015 poem "I Am News" (Part 4).

Bedtime

Translated by Anna Krushelnitskaya

Look, the lights are being lit
Round the block.
Almost bedtime.
Let's just sit,
Sit and talk.

All day long,
I never can
Talk to you.
All you have is work to do,
Work to do.

I don't nag you.
I don't bug.
I don't dig.
I just sit here
I just wait,
Acting big . . .

Almost bedtime.
Let's just sit,
Sit and talk,
Watch the streetlights being lit
Round the block.

ALEXANDER RASKIN (1914–1971) was born in Vitebsk, Belarus. He graduated from the Maxim Gorky Literary Institute in Moscow in 1938, before publishing several popular collections of satirical essays and literary parodies. He also wrote plays and film scripts, notably for the movie *Spring* (1947). His unpublished epigrams were well known in literary circles. Raskin was married to the writer and journalist Frida Vigdorova, who recorded the court hearings in the trial of poet Joseph Brodsky in 1964. Raskin's short, humorous stories for children from the collection *When Papa Was Little* (1961), including the story "How Papa Chose His Profession," were written for his daughters and instantly gained wide popularity. Raskin's second collection of stories for children, *How Papa Went to School,* came out in 1963. Both collections have been reprinted multiple times.

How Papa Chose His Profession

Translated by Katherine E. Young

When Papa was little, people often asked him the same question. They'd ask him: "What do you want to be when you grow up?" And Papa always answered the question without a moment's hesitation. But each time, he answered differently. At first Papa wanted to be a night watchman. He really liked the fact that while everyone else was sleeping, a watchman didn't sleep. He also really liked the rattle that the watchman twirled. And being able to make noise while everyone was asleep pleased Papa very much, too. He firmly resolved to be a night watchman when he grew up. But then an ice cream vendor appeared with a beautiful green cart. You could drive the cart! You could eat ice cream!

"I'll sell a serving, and then I'll eat one!" thought Papa. "And I'll give little children free ice cream."

Little Papa's parents were very surprised when they found out that their son would be an ice cream man. They laughed at him for a long time. But he had firmly chosen that happy and delicious profession for himself.

Then one day little Papa saw an amazing person at the train station.

That person played all day with train cars and steam locomotives. Not with toy ones, but real ones! He sprang onto platforms, crawled under train cars, and played a marvelous game the whole time.

"Who's that?" asked Papa.

"That's the car coupler," they told him.

And then little Papa finally understood what he'd be when he grew up. Just think: coupling and uncoupling train cars! Could anything in the world be more interesting than that? Of course, nothing could be more interesting. When Papa announced that he'd be a car coupler for the railroad, someone asked: "But what about ice cream?"

Then Papa had second thoughts. He'd firmly resolved to become a car coupler. But he also didn't want to give up the green cart with ice cream. And then little Papa found a way out.

"I'll be a car coupler and an ice cream man!" he announced.

Everyone was very surprised. But little Papa explained. He said:

"It's really easy. In the morning, I'll walk around with the ice cream. I'll walk around and around, and then I'll run to the train station. I'll couple the train cars and run back to the ice cream. Then I'll run back to the station, uncouple the cars, and run to the ice cream again. And back and forth like that all the time. And I'll leave the cart close to the station, so I don't have to run far to couple and uncouple the cars."

Everyone laughed a lot. Then little Papa got angry and said:

"If you're going to laugh, I'll also work as a night watchman. After all, my nights are free. And I already know how to twirl the rattle. One of the watchmen let me try it . . ."

That's how Papa planned it. But soon afterwards he wanted to be a pilot. Then he wanted to become a performer and go on the stage. Then he visited a factory with his grandfather and decided to become a lathe operator. On top of that, he very much wanted to be a cabin boy on a ship. Or if all else failed, to be a cowherd and amble around with the cows all day long, loudly flicking the whip. And then one day, he wanted more than anything in the world to be a dog. That whole day he ran around on all fours, barking at strangers and even trying to bite an old woman when she wanted to pat him on the head. Little Papa taught himself to bark very well, but he couldn't teach himself to scratch behind his ears with his foot, although he tried with all his might. To get the hang of it, he went out into the yard and sat next to Tuzik. An unfamiliar military man was walking along the street. The military man stopped and began watching Papa. He watched and watched and then asked:

"What are you doing, young man?"

"I want to be a dog," said little Papa.

Then the unfamiliar military man asked:

"Don't you want to be a person?"

"I've already been a person for a long time!" said Papa.

"What kind of person are you," said the military man, "if you can't even be a good dog? Are real people like that?"

"What kind of a person am I?" asked Papa.

"Think about it!" said the military man, and he walked away.

He wasn't laughing one bit, and not even smiling.

But for some reason, little Papa became very ashamed. And he began to think. He thought and thought, and the more he thought, the more ashamed he grew. The military man hadn't explained anything to him. But he suddenly understood that you couldn't choose a new profession every day.

And most importantly, he understood that he was still little and that he didn't yet know what he'd be when he grew up.

When they asked him about it again, he remembered the military man and said:

"I'll be a person!"

And nobody laughed at that.

And little Papa understood that that was the most correct answer.

And he still thinks so now. First and foremost, you have to be a good person. That's the most important thing for a pilot, a lathe operator, a cowherd, and a performer. And people have absolutely no need to scratch behind their ears with their feet.

VIKTOR DRAGUNSKY (1913–1972) was born in New York City to a family of Jewish immigrants. In 1914, a year after his birth, the family returned to Russia, where his stepfather was the director of a traveling Jewish musical theater. Dragunsky began acting at an early age and performed in theaters, the circus, and in movies. In the 1940s, he began publishing satirical stories and writing songs, parodies, and dialogs for the theater and circus. Dragunsky took part in the volunteer corps during World War II, and later worked as a clown entertaining the troops. In 1944, he became a clown in the Tverskoy Boulevard Moscow Circus. Later, Dragunsky wrote a book about the first days of the war titled *He Fell on the Grass* (1963). In 1959, Dragunsky began writing a series of humorous short stories about two friends, Denis Korablev and Mishka Slonov, titled *The Adventures of Deniska*. The hero, Deniska, was named after Dragunsky's son, Denis. In the 1960s and 1970s, Dragunsky published several short story collections about the two boys, on which many later movies were based. "The Main Rivers," one of the Deniska stories, was first published in 1963. *The Adventures of Deniska* continues to be republished today and has been translated into many languages.

The Main Rivers

Translated by Katya Farber

Although I am already almost nine, it only hit me yesterday that you really do need to do your homework. Like it or not, want to or not, lazy or not, you have to study. It's the law. Because otherwise you can land in such a big mess that you won't even be able to dig yourself out. I, for example, didn't have time to do my homework yesterday. We were assigned to memorize part of a Nekrasov poem and the main rivers of America. And I, instead of studying, was in the yard flying a kite to space. The kite didn't make it to space, but that's because its tail was way too light, so it just spun like a top. That was the first problem. Second, I didn't have a lot of string, so I searched the whole house and gathered everything I could find. I even took the threads from my mom's sewing machine and even that wasn't enough. The kite made it as high as the roof and froze, which is not nearly far enough to reach space.

And I was so busy with that kite and with space that I completely forgot about everything in the world. Playing was so interesting that I stopped thinking about any kind of homework. It completely left my mind. Turns out, you're absolutely not allowed to forget your work, because it will only bring embarrassment.

In the morning I slept in a bit, and when I leapt up there was only a tiny bit of time left. I had read earlier how efficiently firefighters get dressed—they don't waste even a single movement—and I liked that so much that I spent half the summer practicing getting ready quickly. And today when I sprung up and looked at the clock, I immediately realized that I needed to get ready like a firefighter. So today I got fully dressed in one minute and forty-eight seconds, properly, except that I laced my boots through every other hole. Anyways, I made it to school on time and to class a second before Raisa Ivanovna. Meaning that she was walking normally through the corridor, and I was running from the coatroom (everyone had already left it). When I saw her from afar, I ran with all my might, and, still about 5 steps away from the classroom, I swerved around Raisa Ivanovna and leapt into the class. I beat her by about a second and a half, and when she entered, my books were already in my desk and I was sitting with Mishka like nothing had even happened. Raisa Ivanovna entered, and we all got up and said hello, with me being the loudest so she would see how polite I was. But she didn't notice and only said:

"Korablev, to the board!"

My mood immediately soured because I remembered that I had forgotten to prepare for class. And I really didn't want to crawl out from behind my wonderful desk. It was like I was glued to it. But Raisa Ivanovna started hurrying me:

"Korablev! Don't you hear that I'm calling on you?"

So, I went up to the desk. Raisa Ivanovna said:

"The poem!"

I was to recite the poem that was assigned. But I didn't know it. I didn't even really know which one was assigned. So, I paused, hoping that maybe Raisa Ivanovna had also forgotten which one was assigned and wouldn't pay attention to what I was reading. So, I boldly started:

> Winter! . . . The countryman, enchanted,
> breaks a new passage with his sleigh;
> his nag has smelt the snow, and planted
> a shambling hoof along the way.[5]

"That's Pushkin," Raisa Ivanovna said.

"Yes," I said, "it's Pushkin. Alexander Sergeevich."

"And what did I assign?" she asked.

"Yes!" I said.

"What do you mean, 'yes'? What did I assign? Korablev!"

"What?" I said.

"What 'what'? I'm asking, what did I assign?"

Then Mishka made an innocent face and asked, "Doesn't he know that you assigned Nekrasov? He just didn't understand the question, Raisa Ivanovna."

That's what it means to be a loyal friend. That's how Mishka sneakily managed to give me a hint. By that point Raisa Ivanovna was already mad.

"Slonov! Don't you dare prompt him!"

"Yeah," I said. "Why are you interfering, Mishka? What, like without you I don't know that Raisa Ivanovna assigned us Nekrasov! I was just thinking that, and you're just butting in and messing me up."

Mishka blushed and turned away. And I was again left on my own with Raisa Ivanovna.

"Well?" She said.

"What?" I said.

---

5 Translation by Charles H. Johnston.

"Stop fooling around!"

I could tell that she was really angry by now.

"Recite it. By heart!"

"What?" I said.

"The poem, of course!" She said.

"Oh right, got it. So, the poetry then?" I said. "I can do that." I loudly started: "The poem of Nekrasov. A poet. A great poet."

"Go on!" Said Raisa Ivanovna.

"What?" I said.

"Recite it immediately!" Yelled poor Raisa Ivanovna. "Recite it immediately I'm telling you! The title!"

While she was yelling, Mishka had managed to give me a hint on the first word. He whispered it without opening his mouth, but I understood him completely. That's why I bravely stepped forward and declared:

"Tim . . ."

Everybody went silent, including Raisa Ivanovna. She carefully looked at me, and I was looking at Mishka even more carefully. He was pointing to his thumb.

And I somehow immediately remembered the title and said:

"Dumb . . ."

And then repeated the whole thing:

"Tim Dumb!"

Everybody burst out laughing. Raisa Ivanovna said:

"Enough, Korablev! Don't bother, you won't be able to do it. If you don't know it, don't embarrass yourself." Then she added: "What else do you know? Remember, we all agreed yesterday as a class that we'll read interesting books that are outside the program? Yesterday you all agreed to memorize the rivers of America. Did you learn them?"

Of course, I hadn't learned them. That kite, damn it, completely ruined my life. And I wanted to admit everything to Raisa Ivanovna but instead of that I unexpectedly, even for myself, said:

"Of course, I learned them! Obviously!"

"Well then, fix the awful impression you've left with your reading of Nekrasov's poem. Tell me the biggest river in America, and I'll let you go."

That's when I felt sick. Honestly, even my stomach started hurting. It was surprisingly silent in the class. Everyone was looking at me. And I was looking at the ceiling. And thinking that I would definitely just die on the spot. Goodbye, everyone! And in that second, I noticed that in the last row on the left, Petya Gorbyshkin was showing me some kind of long newspaper ribbon, and there was something thickly smeared on it in ink, he probably finger painted it. And I started carefully looking at those letters and finally read the first half.

And then Raisa Ivanovna again:

"Well, Korablev? What is the biggest river in America?"

I immediately filled up with confidence and said:

"Missi-pissi."

I won't tell you the rest. Enough. And although Raisa Ivanovna laughed until she had tears in her eyes, she still gave me an F. And now I swear I'll always do my homework. Until I'm old and gray.

VIKTOR GOLYAVKIN (1929–2001) was a writer and an artist. Born in Baku, Azerbaijan, he studied art in Samarkand and Dushanbe, and was trained as an artist at the Academy of Art in Leningrad. Golyavkin published short, humorous stories for children in the magazines *Campfire* and *Murzilka*. His first book of short stories, *Notebooks in the Rain,* was published in 1959. His most famous book, *My Kind Papa,* came out in 1964, and included the story "On the Balcony." The book became the basis for a film of the same title released in 1970. Golyavkin later published short stories for adult readers; by the end of his career he had produced dozens of collections for children and adults alike.

On the Balcony

Translated by Katherine E. Young

I go out on the balcony. I see a girl with a bow in her hair. She lives in the building over the way. I could whistle at her. She'd look up and see me. That's what I want. "Hey," I'll say, "Tra-la-la, tri-li-li!" She'll say: "Idiot!" or something like that. And she'll keep on walking. As if nothing had happened. As if I hadn't made fun of her. Who does she think she is? What do I care about a bow? As if I were waiting for her! I'm waiting for Papa. He'll bring me presents. He'll tell me about war. And about olden times. Papa knows so many stories. No one could possibly tell better ones. I could listen to them over and over!

Papa knows about everything in the world. But sometimes he doesn't want to tell me things. Then he's sad, and he keeps saying: "No, I wrote it wrong, not that way, the music's wrong . . . But you," he says to me, "you won't let me down, will you?"

I don't want to hurt Papa's feelings. He dreams that I'll become a composer. I stay quiet. I don't care about music. He understands.

"That's sad," he says. "You can't even imagine how sad that is!"

Why is it sad, when I'm not sad at all? After all, Papa doesn't wish anything bad for me. So why does he say that?

"What will you be when you grow up?" he says.

"A general," I say.

"War, again?" Papa is unhappy. But he went to war himself. He galloped on a horse, shot a machine gun . . .

My papa is very kind. One day my brother and I say to Papa: "Buy us ice cream, lots and lots, so we can eat our fill!"

"Here's a dishpan," says Papa, "Run and get some ice cream."

Mama says: "But they'll catch colds!"

"It's summer now," Papa answers. "How can they catch colds?"

"But the throat, the throat," says Mama.

Papa says: "Everyone has a throat. Everyone still eats ice cream."

"But not that much!" says Mama.

"Let them eat as much as they want. It doesn't matter how much! They won't eat more than they're able." That's what Papa says.

And we take the dishpan and go to get ice cream. And we bring it back full. We put the dishpan on the table. The sun shines through the window. The ice cream begins to melt. Papa says: "That's summer for you," and tells us to get spoons and sit down at the table. We all sit at the table—me, Papa, Mama, and Boba. Boba and I are in seventh heaven! Ice cream flows down our faces, over our shirts. We have such a kind papa! He buys us so much ice cream! So much that now we won't want any more for a long time . . .

Papa planted twenty trees on our street. Now they've grown. There's a giant tree in front of the balcony. If I reach out, I can touch a branch.

I'm waiting for Papa. He'll show up soon. It's hard for me to look through the branches. They hide the street. But I lean down, and I can see the whole street.

KIR BULYCHEV (Igor Mozheiko, 1934–2003) was a science-fiction writer, translator, and historian. Born in Moscow, he received graduate training as a specialist in Burmese history and spent several years in Burma. He translated fiction from several languages, including the works of Arthur C. Clark, Graham Greene, Clifford D. Simak, Ursula K. Le Guin, Georges Simenon, and Jorge Luis Borges. His first science-fiction novel was published in 1965 under his pen name, a combination of his wife's first name, Kira, and his mother's maiden name. Bulychev is best known for his series of novels, novellas, and short stories about Alisa Selezneva, a heroine named after his daughter, Alisa. A girl from the future and a daughter of a space biologist, Alisa travels through space and time. The first book in the series is titled *The Girl for Whom Nothing Goes Wrong* (1965), and the story "Bronty" is from that collection. The animated film *The Mystery of the Third Planet* (1981) and the five-part series *Guest from the Future* (1985) were based on the Alisa books and became very popular Soviet children's entertainment. Bulychev wrote his last book in the Alisa series in 2003 shortly before his death. He also wrote other science-fiction cycles, including *Veliky Guslar* and *Doctor Pavlysh*, and published a number of scholarly works as a historian. He received several Russian and international book prizes for his work, including the USSR State Prize, and helped establish the Alisa Prize in 2001, which is awarded annually to the best Russian work of science fiction and fantasy for children and teens.

Bronty

Translated by Sibelan Forrester

They brought a brontosaurus egg to us in the Moscow Zoo. Some Chilean tourists had found the egg; it had been buried by a landslide on the shore of the Yenisei River. The egg was almost spherical and wonderfully preserved by the permafrost. When the specialists examined it, they discovered that the egg was quite fresh. Therefore, they decided to put it in the zoo's incubator. Of course, no one thought this would succeed, but a week later, x-rays showed that the brontosaurus embryo was already developing. No sooner was this announced on intervideo than scientists and journalists started flying to Moscow from every direction. We had to reserve all eighty floors of the Venus Hotel on Tverskaya Street. And even that couldn't hold them all. Eight Turkish paleontologists were sleeping on my dining room floor, I bedded down in the kitchen with a journalist from Ecuador, and two correspondents from the magazine *Women of the Antarctic* set up camp in Alisa's bedroom.

When mom videophoned us in the evening from Nukus, where she was at work building a stadium, she thought she had called the wrong number.

All the telesatellites were showing the egg. The egg in profile, the egg straight on, the egg alongside brontosaurus skeletons . . .

An entire conference of cosmophilologists made a field trip to the zoo. But by that time we had already stopped allowing access to the incubator, and the philologists had to look at the polar bears and Martian praying mantises.

On the forty-sixth day of this crazy life the egg gave a twitch. At that moment my friend Professor Yakata and I were sitting by the protective hood that covered the egg and drinking tea. We had already stopped believing that anything would hatch out of the egg. We had stopped x-raying it, so as not to harm our "baby." And we couldn't make any predictions, since after all no one before us had ever tried to hatch brontosauri.

So, the egg twitched, twitched again . . . cracked, and a black head like a snake's came poking through the thick leathery shell. The automatic cameras started clicking. I knew that the red light had turned on over the door of the incubator. Something very much like a panic began on the zoo grounds.

Five minutes later everyone who had some business being here had gathered around us, plus many who were not at all obligated to be here, but really wanted to be. It immediately got very hot inside.

At last a little baby brontosaurus climbed out of the egg.

"Papa, what's his name?" I suddenly heard a familiar voice.

"Alisa!" I said in surprise. "How did you get here?"

"I'm with the correspondents."

"But children aren't allowed in here."

"I'm allowed. I told everyone that I'm your daughter. And they let me come in."

"You do know that it's not good to take advantage of connections for personal purposes?"

"But, Papa, little Bronty might be bored without any kids, so that's why I came."

I just shrugged. I didn't have a single free minute to walk Alisa home from the incubatorium. And there was no one around who would have agreed to do it for me.

"Stay here and don't go anywhere," I told her, and I rushed to the hood with the newborn brontosaurus.

Alisa and I didn't talk to each other all evening. We had disagreed. I told her not to show up any more at the incubator, but she said she couldn't obey me because she was sorry for Bronty. The next day too she made her way to the incubator. The cosmonauts from the "Jupiter-8" spaceship brought her in. The cosmonauts were heroes, and no one could say no to them.

"Good morning, Bronty," she said, stepping up to the hood.

The little brontosaurus looked sideways at her.

"Whose child is that?" Professor Yakata asked severely.

The earth almost swallowed me up.

But Alisa is never at a loss for words.

"Don't you like me?" she asked.

"No, what do you mean, quite the opposite . . . I just thought that maybe you had lost your way." The professor had no idea how to converse with little girls.

"All right," said Alisa. "I'll come see you tomorrow, Bronty. Don't be sad."

And indeed, Alisa did come the next day. And she came almost every day. Everyone got used to her and let her in without any conversations. I washed my hands of the business. After all, our house was next door to the zoo, she didn't need to cross any streets, and she always had someone to walk with.

The brontosaurus grew quickly. After a month he was eight feet long, and we moved him to a specially constructed pavilion. The brontosaurus wandered through the fenced-in enclosure and chewed on bamboo shoots and bananas. The bamboo was delivered by freight rocket from India, while the bananas were supplied to us by farmers in Malakhovka. Brackish water splashed in the cement pool in the middle of the enclosure. That's how the brontosaurus liked it. But then he suddenly lost his appetite. For three days the bamboo and bananas lay there untouched. On the fourth day the brontosaurus lay down on the bottom of the pool and laid his little head on the plastic rim. It was obvious that he was getting ready to die. We couldn't let this happen. After all, we had only one brontosaurus. The best doctors in the world were trying to help us. But all in vain. Bronty refused grass, vitamins, oranges, and milk—everything.

Alisa didn't know anything about this tragedy. I had sent her off to visit her grandmother in Vnukovo. But on the fourth day she happened to turn on the television just as they were reporting on the brontosaurus's health issues. I have no idea how she talked her grandmother into it, but that very morning she came running into the pavilion.

"Papa!" she shouted. "How could you keep this secret from me? How could you?"

"Later, Alisa, later," I said. "We're having a meeting."

We were in fact really having a meeting. It had been going on for the past three days. Alisa said nothing and walked away. But another minute later I heard someone gasp next to me. I turned around and saw that Alisa had already climbed over the barrier, slipped into the enclosure and run up to the brontosaurus's muzzle. She had a white bread roll in her hand.

"Eat this, Bronty," she said, "or they'll starve you to death here. If I were you, I'd be tired of bananas too."

And before I could make it to the barrier, something unbelievable happened. Something that made Alisa famous and seriously undermined the reputation of us biologists.

The brontosaurus raised its head, took a look at Alisa, and carefully took the bread out of her hands.

"Shush, Papa," Alisa shook her finger at me when she saw I was about to jump over the barrier. "Bronty is scared of you."

"He will not do anything to harm her," said Professor Yakata.

I could see for myself that he wouldn't do anything to harm her. But what if Grandma got a look at this scene?

Afterwards the scientists debated for a long time. They're debating up to the present day. Some say Bronty needed a change in diet, others say that he trusted Alisa more than us. But one way or the other, the crisis passed.

Now Bronty has grown entirely tame. He's nearly a hundred feet long, but there's nothing he likes better than giving Alisa a ride. One of my assistants built a special stepladder, and when Alisa comes into the pavilion, Bronty reaches into the corner with his lo-o-ong neck, picks up the stepladder standing there with his triangular teeth, and neatly sets it down against his gleaming black side. Then he gives Alisa a ride around the pavilion or swims with her in the pool.

EMMA MOSHKOVSKAYA (1926–1981), a children's poet and writer, was born and lived her entire life in Moscow. She graduated from the Gnesin School of Music in Moscow and was a singer at the Moscow Conservatory. She published her first poems for children in *Murzilka* and *Pioneer,* for which she received positive reviews from Kornei Chukovsky and Samuil Marshak. She was a prolific children's writer and regularly published her poetry, releasing eight books of children's poems in 1962 alone. Some of her poems became children's songs scored by well-known composers and performed by Russian rock stars. Her poems "I Was Very Mean to My Mommy" and "Clever Old Ladies" were written in the late 1960s, the latter becoming the title work of a collection. Her book *Tales of Little Goat and Little Donkey* (1971) consists of a mixture of poetry and prose.

I Was Very Mean to My Mommy

Translated by Anna Krushelnitskaya

I was very mean to my mommy,
And now we will never be close!
Wherever she goes, I'm not coming.
She'll never bring me where she goes.
She won't wave to me from the window.
I won't wave to her, as well.
I won't ever tell her where I go.
She'll also have nothing to tell.
I'll throw a big sack on my back,
I'll scrounge and I'll find me some bread,
I'll pick the best stick from the stack
And be off to the dark woods ahead!
I will track tigers and beavers,
I will go searching for ore,
I'll build bridges spanning big rivers,
No matter how wildly they roar!
They'll make me the big boss there.
My beard will grow shaggy and long.
I will be so sad and so lost there.
I will be so silent and strong.
But then, one dark night in winter,
After so many years go by,
My mommy will buy a plane ticket,
And she'll get ready to fly.
And then, right on my birthday evening,
The plane will land where I'll be.
My mom will deplane and forgive me.
My mom will be friends with me.

Clever Old Ladies

Translated by Dmitri Manin

I think that old ladies
Keep toys at the ready!
Matryoshkas and Teddies
Are stashed in their caddies.
These clever old ladies
Hide away their caddies,
As they sit in their rockers
Knitting wool stockings
And heaving feigned sighs,
With a cat by their side.
But once home alone,
They don't sigh, they don't groan!
Right then and there
They kick the chair!
No more rocking!
They toss the stocking
And fetch from the caddies
Dolls, lions, and teddies.
From under the pillows
Come clowns and Godzillas.
But if someone comes knocking—
They pick up the stocking . . .
They think no one knows they play
Whenever we go away—
No one in the house, no one
Anywhere under the sun!

Tales of Little Goat and Little Donkey [excerpt]

Translated by Dmitri Manin

The Second Tale

The Little Goat went and met the Little Donkey.
One asked a question, and the other responded:
"Are you happy when someone loves you tenderly?"
"Of course, I am!"
"Does it feel nice?"
"It sure does! It feels marvelous!
If you're handsome and brave,
then you're happy and loved."
"But I'm not handsome . . . not brave . . ."
"Silly! Don't you know
that I love you just so?"

The Little Donkey became the Little Goat's very best friend. One day they were together up until lunchtime. The Little Donkey said:

"Bye-bye! Because I'm leaving if you don't give me this beetle."

"But I *will* give you this beetle."

And so, the Little Donkey didn't leave, but took the blue beetle and pulled its leg off.

"Bye-bye!" said the Little Donkey. "Because I'm leaving if you don't give me this whistle."

"But I *will* give you this whistle," the Little Goat said. And the Little Donkey took it and whistled so that everybody jumped.

"Bye-bye!" said the Little Donkey. "Because I'm leaving if you don't give me that banana up there on your plate."

"But I *will* give you this banana. And another one, and an apple, and candy on top!"

And so, the Little Donkey was with the Little Goat all the way up to lunchtime.

After lunch they were going for a walk in the winter woods.

"I'll be warm," the Little Goat thought, "if I wear my jacket."

And so, he put his jacket on.

"I'll be warm because I have a jacket on! But the jacket," the Little Goat thought, "but my jacket will be cold!" And he pulled a sweater on top of his jacket.

"I'll be warm, the jacket will be warm! But the sweater . . . the sweater will be cold!" thought the Little Goat. And so, he pulled a puffer on top of the sweater.

"I'll be warm, the jacket will be warm, the sweater will be warm! But my puffer . . . But . . . the puffer will be cold!" thought the Little Goat. And so, he pulled a fur coat on top of the puffer.

"I'll be warm, the jacket will be warm, the sweater will be warm, the puffer will be warm! But my fur coat . . . but my fur coat will be cold!" thought the Little Goat. And so, he threw a blanket on top of the fur coat.

"I'll be warm, the jacket will be warm, the sweater will be warm, the puffer will be warm, the fur coat will be warm! But the blanket . . . my fleece blanket, my poor old fleece blanket! . . ." The Little Goat grunted, groaned, and fell on the floor, and didn't go any-any-anywhere at all.

And so, the Little Donkey went alone.

When the Little Donkey came back from the forest, the Little Goat asked him with great interest:

"So, what's there in the forest?"

"Trees."

"What else?"

"Trees."

"And what else?"

"I looked up and saw trees, I looked down and saw trees, and nothing else, trees are all there is . . ."

"What about silence?"

"Yes, there's silence."

"What about whiteness?"

"Yes, there's whiteness."

"And what about the blankets?"

"What blankets?"

"Haven't you seen them?"

"I haven't seen them. There's a lot of snow, but blankets?! No."

"From the top of the crown to the last pinkie twig every tree wears white blankets, some tiny, some big!"

"How do you know, Little Goat?"

"Actually, I don't know!"

But . . . somehow I know, said the Little Goat wondering at himself.

Once there lived a Little Gray Goat
Wee small tiny Little Gray Goat.
Believe it or not,
The Little Gray Goat resolved to become a great hero,
A humongous hero, an unheard-of hero,
An amazing and marvelous hero.
The Little Gray Goat didn't want to sit quiet,
He wanted to take on the Wolf in a fight.
Click-clack the tooth, hop-hop the hoof!
The Little Gray Goat ran from the Wolf.
The Hedgehog said, "Think what you will,
But when chased by the wolves just put up your quills."
"Quills? I don't have them, and I cannot sting,
That's the thing, dear friend Hedgehog."
"Ribbit-ribbit," croaked the Frog,
"Come, Little Goat, jump in the bog!
Here you'll be safe and soaked."
"Sorry, Mrs. Frog, I won't.
A bog isn't good for a goat.
I don't want to live that way
Even for a single day . . ."
Click-clack the tooth, hop-hop the hoof!
The Little Grey Goat ran from the Wolf.
The Big Gray Wolf was catching up.
The Little Gray Goat could barely hop.
Just then he saw a Bear, and so said the Bear:
"Little Goat, come in and be safe in my lair!
Have a treat and tell me a bedtime story."
"Which story, Uncle Bear?" "Make one up on the fly,
You can do it, and I—I won't even try,
It's so incredibly hard!" "All right!
It's really easy, and it's such a delight!
Not a big deal, I have plenty to share!"
And the Little Goat's tales never bored the Great Bear . . .

EDUARD USPENSKY (1937–2018) was born in Yegoryevsk near Moscow. A prolific author of children's books, a playwright, and a television anchor, he created many beloved characters, including Cheburashka, Crocodile Gena, Uncle Fedya, and Postman Pechkin. Among his most famous books are *Crocodile Gena and His Friends* (1966), *Uncle Fedya, His Dog, and His Cat* (1974), *The Little Warranty People* (1975), and *Down the Magic River* (1979). Many of his works have been translated into other languages, gaining popularity all over the world. Uspensky also wrote dozens of scripts for animated films, some based on his own stories. He published a volume of children's horror stories with Andrei Usachev called *Terrifying Children's Folklore* (1998). Uspensky has received several medals and literary prizes, including the 2009 Chukovsky Prize and the 2015 Lev Kopelev Prize for Human Rights. The protagonist of *Uncle Fedya, His Dog, and His Cat* is a precocious boy who runs away from home because his parents will not let him have a cat. He settles in the village of Prostokvashino with his cat Matroskin and a dog named Sharik. The three friends find a buried treasure, and with their newfound wealth buy a tractor that runs on potatoes, which they name Tr-tr Mitya. They live happily in the village until Uncle Fedya falls ill and his parents come to rescue him. This book and its sequels were the basis of three popular animated films released in between 1978 and 1984, which are still enjoyed by Russian-speaking children to this day.

Uncle Fedya, His Dog, and His Cat [excerpts]

Translated by Michael Henry Heim[6]

Chapter 1. Uncle Fedya

There once was a little boy named Fedya. His mother and father called him *Uncle* Fedya because he was so serious. He could read by the time he was four and make soup by the time he was six.

He was a good little boy, and his parents loved him.

Uncle Fedya's only problem was this: His mother didn't like animals, especially cats. And because Uncle Fedya loved animals, he and his mother often quarreled.

One day Uncle Fedya was walking downstairs eating a sandwich when he saw a cat sitting on a windowsill. A big cat. A gigantic tabby cat.

"Uncle Fedya," the cat called, "that's no way to eat a sandwich. The meat never touches your tongue. Take off the bottom slice of bread. Eat the sandwich meat-side down. It'll taste better."

Uncle Fedya tried it. His sandwich did taste better. He gave the cat a bite and asked, "How did you know my name?"

"I live in the attic. I can see everyone in the house from up there. Unfortunately, my attic is closed for repairs at the moment and I have nowhere to live."

"Who taught you to speak?" Uncle Fedya asked.

"Oh, I picked up a word here and there," the cat replied. "And I once lived with a professor who studied animal language. You're lost without language nowadays. You could be made into a hat or a collar or even a doormat."

"Come and live with me," Uncle Fedya suggested.

"I don't know," said the cat. "Wouldn't your mother chase me away?"

"No, Papa wouldn't let her."

So they went upstairs to Uncle Fedya's room.

Uncle Fedya gave the cat a good meal. Then it curled up under the bed and slept for the rest of the day.

The minute Uncle Fedya's parents came home from work that evening there was trouble. "I smell a cat," his mother said. "I bet Uncle Fedya has brought one home with him."

"What if he has?" said his father. "Cats don't bother anybody!"

---

6 Reprinted with permission from Eduard Uspensky, *Uncle Fedya, His Dog, and His Cat*, trans. Michael Henry Heim (Alfred A. Knopf: New York, 1993), 3-18.

"They bother me," his mother said.

"How?"

"They just do. What's the use of having a cat?"

"What's the use of having a cat?" his father said. "What's the use of having that picture on the wall?"

"The use of having that picture on the wall," his mother replied, "is to hide the hole in the wallpaper."

"All right," his father said, "we will *make* a use for it. We will train it to be a dog. It will be our watch-cat and stand guard at the door. It won't bark, it won't bite, but it won't let anybody in."

"You and your ideas!" his mother cried. "Always spoiling the boy!" She was angry now. "This time I'm not giving in. You'll have to choose. It's me or the cat." She turned to see the tabby cat at the bottom of the stairs.

Uncle Fedya's father looked at Uncle Fedya's mother. Then he looked at the cat. Then he looked at each of them again.

"I choose you," he said to Uncle Fedya's mother. "I've known you for ages. I've never seen the cat before."

"What about you, Uncle Fedya?" she asked the boy. He had come into the room when he heard his parents arguing. "Whom do you choose?"

"I can't choose," he answered. "But if the cat goes, I go."

"That's your affair," she said. "I want that cat out of here by tomorrow."

Of course, she never dreamed Uncle Fedya would run away. His father didn't either. But Uncle Fedya meant what he said.

Just before bedtime he put everything he needed into his backpack: a penknife, a flashlight, a change of clothes, and all the money he'd saved up. Then he found a bag for the cat. It fit the creature perfectly—only its whiskers stuck out. And then he went to bed.

The next morning Uncle Fedya's parents went off to work, and Uncle Fedya made himself some breakfast.

After he and the cat had eaten their fill, he wrote the following letter:

Dear Mother and Father,

I love both of you very much. I love animals, too. Especially cats. You won't let me keep the cat I found. I think that's unfair. So I am going to live in the country. Don't worry about me. I can take care of myself, and I'll write often.

Good-bye for now.

Your son,
Uncle Fedya

He left the letter on the kitchen table, hoisted the backpack onto his back, picked up the cat in the bag, and set off for the bus stop.

Chapter 2. In the Country

Uncle Fedya climbed onto the bus and off they went. At that time of day buses to the country were nearly empty. Uncle Fedya and his cat could talk as much as they pleased.

"What's your name?" he asked.

"I don't rightly know," the cat answered. "I've been called Tigerkins and Fluff Ball and Pretty Kitty. I've even been known as Silly Puss. But none of them suits my fancy. I need a new name."

"What kind?"

"Something dignified. And something to do with the sea. My grandmother and grandfather were ship's cats. I'd give anything to set sail. If only I weren't afraid of water," the cat said.

"I know what I'll call you," said Uncle Fedya. "Mr. Matroskin." He chose the name Matroskin because it comes from the Russian word for "sailor."

"That's perfect."

"Besides, you've got stripes like a sailor's suit."

"Yes, Mr. Matroskin suits me fine—very dignified, very seagoing."

The cat was so happy with his new name that he positively grinned. Then he ducked into his bag and tried it out on himself.

"Mr. Matroskin is wanted on the telephone! Mr. Matroskin to the telephone!"

"I'm sorry. Mr. Matroskin is unable to come to the telephone. Mr. Matroskin is extremely busy lying on the stove."

The more he used it, the more he liked it.

"Yes, Mr. Matroskin will most definitely do," the cat said, sticking his head out of the bag. "It's not an ordinary silly name like Alexandrov and Nikolov."

"What's so silly about Alexandrov and Nikolov?" Uncle Fedya asked.

"If your name is Alexandrov people say, 'Alexandrov, take your hand off!' And if your name is Nikolov, people say, 'Nikolov, take your pickle off!'"

Just then the bus came to a halt. They were in the country.

The country was a beautiful place—all woods and fields and running streams, a nice warm breeze, no flies to speak of, and very few people. Uncle Fedya went up to a little old man and asked him, "Is there an empty house nearby? A place where I might live?"

"There are plenty of empty houses here," the old man replied. "They've just put up a five-story apartment building across the river, the kind you see in the city. Half the village lives there now. Left their houses. Left their gardens. Even left a few chickens here and there. Take any house you like. They're yours for the asking."

So off they went. Before they had gone very far, a dog came up to them. He was a shaggy dog, his fur all rumpled and full of prickles.

"Let me live with you," he said. "I'll be your watchdog."

Mr. Matroskin did not like the idea. "We have nothing to watch," he said. "We haven't even got a house yet. Come back in a year when we're rich."

But Uncle Fedya said, "Hush, cat! A good dog never bothered a soul. I wonder where *he* learned to talk."

"Oh, I was once the watchdog of a professor who was studying animal language."

"That must be *my* professor," cried the cat. "He had a wife and two children. He had a cleaning lady with a broom. And his lifework was to write a People-Cat dictionary."

"People-*Cat*?" said the dog. "When I was with him, he was working on a People-*Dog* dictionary. And the cleaning lady had a vacuum cleaner instead of a broom."

"Well, I'm sure he's the same professor," said the cat.

"Where is he now?" asked Uncle Fedya.

"Africa. He's switched to elephants. I stayed behind with the cleaning lady, but we didn't get along. I like people with happy, sausage personalities, and hers was gloomy and broomstick."

"I remember," said the cat. "Gloom and broom."

"Well, what do you say? Will you take me now, or shall I come back in a year?"

"Now!" cried Uncle Fedya. "The more the merrier. What's your name?"

"Sharik," the dog said modestly. Sharik, which means "little ball" in Russian, is the most common name for a Russian dog. "I'm not what you'd call a thoroughbred," he added.

"My name is Uncle Fedya, and this is Mr. Matroskin."

"Pleased to meet you," Sharik said, and bowed.

"What can you do besides guard houses?" asked the cat, still unhappy at the prospect of a dog companion. "A lock can guard a house as well as a dog."

"I can dig up potatoes with my hind paws and wash the dinner dishes with my tongue. And you do not need to give me a place to sleep. I can sleep outdoors." He was very much afraid they wouldn't let him stay.

But all Uncle Fedya said was "Time to find a house. Each of us will pick one, and then we'll decide whose is best."

So they went their separate ways each hoping to find the best house. They all came back bursting with excitement.

"Wait till you see my house!" cried Mr. Matroskin. "There's not a crack in it, and the stove will keep us warm as toast!"

"Stove!" cried Sharik. "Who cares about stoves? Wait till you see *mine*! The doghouse alone is big enough for the three of us."

"Well, *I've* found a house with a television set," said Uncle Fedya. "It has big windows, a solid roof and a vegetable garden. Want to see it?"

As they walked up the front path, Sharik cried, "This one is mine! See the doghouse?"

"No, it's mine." Mr. Matroskin exclaimed as they went inside. "See the stove?"

"Well, well!" said Uncle Fedya." We really have picked the best house."

The more they saw, the better they liked the house. It had everything—a stove and beds and curtains, and a radio and a new television set. The kitchen had pots and pans galore. As for the garden, well, it needed work. It hadn't been weeded in ages. But there were potatoes, carrots, and cabbages everywhere. And there was a fishing rod in the shed.

The first thing Uncle Fedya did was go down to the river to catch some fish. Meanwhile, Sharik and Mr. Matroskin made a fire in the fireplace and hauled in water. They ate, listened to the radio for a while, and went to bed. They were all very happy with their new house.

Chapter 3. New Worries

The next morning Uncle Fedya and his dog and cat tidied up the house. They brushed away the cobwebs, cleaned the stove, and took out the trash.

Mr. Matroskin worked hardest of all. Cats love to have things clean. He dusted all the cupboards and swept under every table, chair, and sofa with his tail. When he had finished, the house positively shone.

Sharik, on the other hand, was almost no help. All he did was tear from corner to corner, barking and sniffing. Finally Uncle Fedya couldn't stand it any longer. He sent Sharik into the garden to dig potatoes. Sharik soon got into the swing of it, and dirt flew in all directions.

It took them the whole day. When the house itself was clean, they weeded the carrot patch and the potatoes, too.

Their work done, they went down to the river for a bath. Sharik needed it most.

"I've never seen a dog so dirty and bedraggled!" said Uncle Fedya. "Into the water with you."

"Fine," said Sharik, "but I can't do it myself. The soap slips out of my mouth. And what's a bath without soap!" So he jumped into the water and Uncle Fedya lathered up his coat.

Meanwhile, Mr. Matroskin walked up and down the riverbank at a safe distance. His ancestors were ship's cats, but he was still afraid of water.

They walked home slowly drying off in the sun. All at once a man ran up to them. He had a red face and a cap on his head. He was about fifty years old.

"What are you doing here?" the man asked. "Who are you, anyway?"

"I'm me, myself, and I," Uncle Fedya answered, "and I've come from the city to be in the county. I'm here on my own."

The man in the cap looked very surprised.

"Children aren't supposed to be on their own," he said. "Children are supposed to be with somebody."

"He is with somebody," said Mr. Matroskin. "Me!"

"And me!" said Shank.

The man in the cap didn't know what to think.

He'd never heard a cat or a dog talk before. There was mischief afoot—that was certain. And then the little boy began asking *him* questions!

"Why do you need to know so much? Are you a police officer?"

The man replied, "I'm not. I am Pechkin, the local postmaster. That's why I need to know so much. If I don't know who you are, I can't deliver your letters and magazines. By the way what magazines do you subscribe to?"

"I've been thinking of trying a children's magazine," said Uncle Fedya.

"And I've been thinking of trying a hunting magazine," said Sharik.

"What about you?" the man asked Mr. Matroskin.

"I've been thinking of saving money," said Mr. Matroskin. "No magazines for me."

GENRIKH SAPGIR (1928–1999) was born in the Siberian town of Biysk. A writer, poet, and translator, he was a part of the Soviet Nonconformist Art movement, the Lionozovo School. In the Soviet period, he was able to publish only his poetry for children; his other poems appeared in émigré magazines and underground collections such as *Continent* and *Metropol*, and were published in Russia only after perestroika. Sapgir was known for his bold experiments in poetry, and was considered one of the best poets of his era. Sapgir constantly created new poetic forms and themes in his cycles, including *Psalms* (1955–1956) and *Sonnets on Shirts*, published in Paris in 1976. Sapgir authored several books for children and dozens of scripts and songs for animated films. Sapgir's children's poetry collections were illustrated by some of the best artists of the time, including the Moscow Conceptualists **Viktor Pivovarov** (b. 1937) and Ilya Kabakov. "Wonder Woods" first appeared in the eponymous collection published in 1967. In 1977, "The Princess and the Ogre" was made into an animated film directed by Eduard Nazarov and voiced by Alexander Gradsky.

Genrikh Sapgir, *Wonder Woods*, illus. Viktor Pivovarov (Moscow-St. Petersburg: Rech', 2013). Courtesy of the Russian State Children's Library.

Wonder Woods

Translated by Dmitri Manin

We'll go, you and I,
To the wonder woods

Where by the lake
Roams the Indigo Moose.
Where the Red Fox sweeps
Every glade and trail
And keeps the woods clean
With its furry tail.
We'll go to the wonder woods,
Where
We'll make friends
With the Clever Bear.

We'll take a peek
In the Owl's nest.
It is warm and neat
And the sheets are pressed.
The Owl's two eyes
Are two room lights,
And she has a soft sofa
For comfy nights.
You and I and the Bear,
We'll sit along
And sing together
The forest song:

Spruce and birch,
Oak and pine,
The sun, the moon
And the stars up high.
Birch and spruce,
Pine and oak,
Sun and rain,
Hail and snow.

We'll make friends with the Owl,
And then
We'll all go
To the Lion's den.
In the hillside
We'll spot a sign

On the door:
"THE GENTLE LION."

The Lion
Is gentle and sweet,
He'll shake your paw
And purr his "GR-R-REET!"
And if you ask him,
If you're polite,
He'll let you pet him
And will not bite.

You can run with the Deer,
Play tag and chase . . .
For the wonder woods
Is an awesome place!
They like to play games
And throw the ball,
There is no
Bullying
Or tussles.
But most of all,
Yes, most of all
They like
Poems
And puzzles!

You and I, we'll go there
Just for fun,
But we'll leave at home
Your old pop gun,
We won't take with us
Your old pop gun,
For the Law of the Land there
Is SCARE NO ONE.

At the edge of the forest
There's a sign: "GUNS ARE BANNED!
NO SLINGSHOTS OR CANNONS

IN THIS FAIRY LAND!
THEY ARE BANISHED FOREVER."

Get ready, my friend,
Let's go, let's go,
Give me your hand!

The Princess and the Ogre

Translated by Dmitri Manin

Here's how it happened:
The Princess was just
adorable,
the weather was simply
horrible.
One day
when all was good
the Princess
got lost in the woods.
Then she saw an adorable
meadow
and a shack there, a horrible
shadow.
Said the Ogre in the shack:
"Come here, baby,
for a snack!"
He grabbed for his knife
—that means trouble!—
then he saw she was really . . .
adorable!
Right away, the Ogre felt
sick.
"Beat it," he said,
"and quick.
Appetite tonight
is horrible,
for the sight isn't right:

too adorable."
And the Princess walked quietly
away
and came back to the castle
that day.
And that's how it ends,
the horrible
legend
of Princess Adorable.

Or perhaps it was the other way around:
The Princess looked simply
horrible,
the weather looked just
adorable.
One day
when all was good
the Princess
got lost in the woods.
Then she saw a horrible
meadow
and a shack, an adorable
shadow.
Said the Ogre in the shack:
"Come here, baby,
for a snack!"
He grabbed for his knife
—that means trouble!—
then he saw she was really . . .
horrible!
Right away, the Ogre felt
sick.
"Beat it," he said,
"and quick.
Appetite tonight
is adorable,
but the sight isn't right:
too horrible."
And the Princess walked quietly

away
and came back to the castle
that day.
And that's how it ends,
the adorable
legend
of Princess Horrible.

SERGEI KOZLOV (1939–2010), a poet, scriptwriter, and author of fairy tales, was born in Moscow. In 1961, he entered the Maxim Gorky Literary Institute, before publishing several collections of tales and poems for children in 1962. He is best known for his story "Hedgehog in the Fog," and for the script of the animated film by the same title directed by Yury Norshtein (1975). The film received the USSR State Prize in 1979 and eighteen international film prizes. In 2003, it was named "the best animated film of all time" at the Laputa Animation Festival in Japan. Francheska Yarbusova was the film's art director, and her illustrations were republished in many editions of the story. Other famous animated films based on Kozlov's scripts are *How Lion Cub and Turtle Sang Together* (1974) and *How Hedgehog and Bearcub Changed the Sky* (1985). Kozlov was nominated for the Hans Christian Andersen Prize in 2006, and he received the Chukovsky Prize in 2009. "Hedgehog in the Fog" and "Hedgehog, Bearcub, and the Dust on the Stars" are the part of the collection *Hedgehog and Bearcub* (1975).

Hedgehog in the Fog

Translated by Alexandra Berlina

Two dozen tiny midges swarmed into the clearing and began playing their squeaky fiddles. The moon came out from behind the clouds and glided across the sky, smiling.

A dog howled. "Mmmoooo!" sighed a cow across the river. The river and the cow were both dappled, the cow with brown spots, the river with three dozen pieces of moonlight.

Fog rose over the river, and a sad, white horse sank in the fog up to its chest. It seemed as if a great white duck was swimming in the whiteness, snorting when the fog got into its nostrils.

Hedgehog was sitting under a pine tree on a hill, looking out over the valley flooded with mist and moonlight.

It was all so beautiful that he wondered: was it perhaps just a dream?

And all the while, the midges kept playing their fiddles, and the dog kept howling, and the silvery dapples kept dancing on the river.

"Can you believe this beauty!" thought Hedgehog, looking ever so closely so that he'd remember it all to the last blade of grass.

"Now, a star has fallen," he whispered, "and the grass is bending to the left, and the fir tree has almost disappeared in the fog, floating there next to the horse . . ."

And then he thought: "Oh, but if the horse falls asleep, won't it drown in the fog?"

And he started down the hill, ever so slowly, right into the fog, so he could see what it was like inside.

"Here I am. I can't see a thing. Not even my own paws," he said. And then he called: "Horse!"

But the horse was silent.

"Horse, where are you?" thought Hedgehog. He took a cautious step forward, then another. Everything was dull and dark and dank, the only faint glow somewhere up high.

Hedgehog padded on and on—and then, all at once, the ground disappeared from under him, and he plummeted down.

Plop!

"I'm in the river!" Hedgehog realized, cold with dread, and he started kicking about.

When he surfaced, he surfaced into the same darkness. He didn't even know where the shore was.

"Let the river carry me!" he decided. He took as deep a breath as he could and floated downstream.

The river rushed its reeds, seethed around the rifts, and Hedgehog felt that he was quite soaked and would soon drown.

It was then that someone touched his paw.

"Excuse me," Someone said silently, "but who are you? How did you get here?"

"I'm Hedgehog," Hedgehog replied, also without words. "I fell into the river."

"Then you should climb onto my back," Someone suggested silently. "I will take you to the shore."

Hedgehog climbed onto Someone's narrow slippery back, and in a minute he was onshore.

"Thank you," he said aloud.

"You're welcome," said the invisible Someone silently, and disappeared into the waves.

"Can you believe this story!" Hedgehog thought, shaking himself off.

And off he waddled through the fog.

Hedgehog, Bearcub, and the Dust on the Stars

Translated by Alexandra Berlina

For a whole month now, Hedgehog has been climbing a pine tree every night to wipe the stars clean.

"If I don't wipe the stars clean every night," he thought, "they'll get all dusty and dull."

So, every morning, he'd step out onto his porch, get some twigs for a fresh broom to dust off the stars before wiping, and wash the cleaning rag. He only had the one rag, so he had to wash it every morning and then hang it on the pine to dry.

Every morning, Hedgehog did all this, and then he ate his lunch and went to bed. By the time he woke up, everything was glittering with evening dew. He had dinner and, moving slowly from branch to branch, climbed to the very top of the pine, rag in one paw and broom in the other.

And then the work began in earnest. First, he'd dust off the stars—very, very gently, lest he knocked them out of the sky. Then he'd put the broom in his left paw, take the rag into the right and wipe the stars to a shine. This was meticulous work, and it took all night.

"Well, someone has to do it, don't they?" Hedgehog grumbled to himself at the top of the pine. "If Bearcub doesn't wipe the stars clean, if I don't wipe the stars clean, then who will wipe them clean?"

All the while, Bearcub, too, would be balancing on top of a pine tree near his own house, wiping the stars and thinking:

"How clever Hedgehog must be to come up with such a wonderful idea! After all, if he hadn't thought of cleaning the stars, they'd have become invisible ages ago. Here, this one is terribly dusty!" And he blew on a star before rubbing it with his rag.

Bearcub tried very hard, but he wasn't quite as good at it as Hedgehog was. So whenever a star fell from the sky, everyone in the forest knew that it was Bearcub who had accidentally knocked it down.

OLEG GRIGORIEV (1943–1992) was born in the Volodga region. A poet and artist, he was an integral part of the Leningrad artistic underground. Grigoriev graduated from Leningrad Art School in 1961, but was later expelled from the Leningrad Academy of Art. He worked as a postman, a seasonal worker, and a yard-keeper. In 1975, Grigoriev exhibited his art at independent shows in Leningrad. Many of his short and darkly humorous poems became oral legends. In 1970, Grigoriev published his first collection of children's poetry, *The Oddballs*. Soon after, he was sentenced to two years of forced labor for being a "parasite"—a Soviet term for people without regular employment. Grigoriev's second collection, *Growth Vitamin*, came out ten years later, and was heavily criticized by the literary establishment. His third collection, *The Talking Raven*, was published in 1987. His 1981 application to the Writers Union was rejected; he became a member only in 1991. Grigoriev's first two books of poetry for adults were published after his death in 1993. His children's poems combine paradoxical images and black humor with a naïve, childlike perspective. The three short poems selected for this volume are from his 1980 collection *Growth Vitamin*, which in 1985 inspired a one-act opera by Leonid Desyatnikov, followed in 1988 by an animated film by Vasily Kafanov.

Something Crawled onto the Table

Translated by Jane Bugaeva

Something crawled onto the table: a bug.
Such a bug, that if you cover it with a mug
the bug would carry away the mug.
The mug would tip over
and it'd all be over
he would escape, that bug, and likely return
to overturn
other mugs.
So instead, I caught the bug
and put it under the rug.
And to stop the bug
from escaping the rug
I covered it with the mug.

My Bicycle Carried Me Away

Translated by Jane Bugaeva

My bicycle carried me away.
It carried me so far astray—
that it lost its wheels,
and with dismay
I carried it the rest of the way.

A Boy Bought Some Bread at the Store

Translated by Jane Bugaeva

A boy bought some bread at the store—
a baguette so long it touched the floor.
He carried it carefully under his arm
while a small ginger pup followed along.
Not once did the boy turn around
while his baguette got whittled down.

IRINA PIVOVAROVA (1939–1986) was a children's poet and book illustrator. Born in Moscow, she received a degree in applied arts from Moscow State Textile University. Later, Pivovarova worked as a set dresser and clothing designer, creating the uniform for the Artek Pioneer Camp. Pivovarova's poems were first published in the magazine *Merry Pictures*. She published more than fifteen volumes of children's short stories, novellas, and poetry, some of which became the basis for animated films. Among Pivovarova's most famous prose collections were *What My Head Is Thinking About, or Stories of Lyusya Sinitsina, a Third Grader* (1975); *The Old Man in Checkered Pants, or Stories of Pavlik Pomidorov, Lyusya Sinitsina's Brother* (1981); and *Katya and Manechka* (1986). Some of her books of poetry were illustrated by her husband, the artist Viktor Pivovarov, one of the leading figures of Soviet "unofficial art" and a prolific illustrator of children's books. "We Searched the World Both Far and Wide" and "When . . ." are from the collection *A Little Half-Moon Goat* (1977). "Teeny Tiny Pony" was first published in *Two Very Brave Rabbits* (1975); "The Violin" first appeared in the collection *Magic Wand* (1978).

We Searched the World Both Far and Wide

Translated by Lydia R. Stone

We searched the world both far and wide
In hopes to find a special treasure.
A little girl who never cried,
A boy who brushed his teeth with pleasure.
Our search was long and hard and lonely
And in the end, we could find only
A little boy who never ever cried,
A girl who brushed her teeth with pride.

When . . .

Translated by Lydia R. Stone

When kids cry in the kitchen
That room will soon be soaked.
Then, In our tear-drenched kitchen,
Bull frogs will start to croak.
And after that our kitchen
With swamp plants will be filled.
To get into our kitchen
A bridge we'll have to build.
That bridge into our kitchen,
Dear guests, we hope you'll cross.
Bring hankies to the kitchen
To dry wet noses off.

Teeny Tiny Pony

Translated by Lydia R. Stone

Teeny tiny pony—
Was extremely cute and sweet
But a problem for his mommy:

For he simply wouldn't eat.
When she served him meals quite yummy,
He just yelled and kicked his feet;
Would he taste them? Nope, nope, nope.
Mommy as a last resort
Hauled him off to Dr. Snort.
The Doctor with his stethoscope
Gently poked at pony's tummy.
Pony jumped up to his feet,
Cried, "I want to eat and eat.
Everything I see looks yummy.
I would even eat that pen,
Or this ticket for bus ten.
That band-aid and that piece of gauze,
Paper cups and plastic straws.
Tongue depressor, rubber glove.
That's the kind of meal I'd love.
After that I'd eat much more.
What's that lying on the floor?"

The Violin

Translated by Lydia R. Stone

The violin, beneath her bow,
Sang songs of sad sweet sorrow
And all who heard that music flow
Her sad mood seemed to borrow.
The violin soon changed her style.
I guess of sadness weary.
And all who heard began to smile,
To hear that music cheery.

PART 4

New Russia, New Stories (1989–2017)

GRIGORY OSTER (b. 1947) was born in Odesa and graduated from the Maxim Gorky Literary Institute in Moscow in 1982. Oster's first volume of children's poetry, *It's So Nice to Give Presents,* was published in 1975, introducing his now famous characters Boa, Baby Elephant, Parrot, and Monkey. Oster has written screenplays for well-known animated series, including *38 Parrots* (1976–1991) and *A Kitten Called Woof* (1977–1980). The first of Oster's signature "bad advice" stories, "The Brave Cook," was published in *Little Bun* magazine in 1983. His first collected volume of bad advice, *Horrible Advice: A Book for Disobedient Children and Their Caregivers,* came out in 1990. Several other books of bad advice followed, including *Mathematical Exercises* (1993) and *Exercises in Physics* (1994), both of which combined humor with instructional materials. Oster authored many more books that employ absurd situations, nonsense, and hyperbole. In 1989, he published a postmodern novel for children titled *A Tale with Details.* Oster's books have sold millions of copies. At the invitation of the Presidential Administration of Russia, Oster took part in the creation of the 2004 website The President of Russia for Schoolchildren. He has received many awards, including the 2002 Russian Federation State Prize and the 2012 Chukovsky Prize. The seven poems included in this volume are from his first *Horrible Advice* collection.

Horrible Advice: A Book for Disobedient Children and Their Caregivers [select poems]

Translated by Jane Bugaeva

Recently, scientists have discovered that the world is full of disobedient children who do exactly the opposite of what they're told.

They're told: "Wash your hands!" and of course, they do not.

They're told: "Remember to say 'Please' and 'Thank you.'" And they forget right away.

It was clear to the scientists that the only way to make these children listen was to stop telling them all the right things to do, and to start telling them all the wrong things to do.

Since these children do the opposite of what they're told, everything works out for the best.

Caught red-handed by your mother
while you're painting passionately
on the walls in your apartment
(something that you're known for doing)
just explain to her quite simply
that you wanted to surprise her
with a portrait that you've titled:
"Mommy Dearest in Profile."

If you're racing down the hallway
on a bike that's new and shiny
and your dad comes out the bathroom
for a little morning stroll,
do not turn into the kitchen
there's a fridge there with sharp corners,
but your dad—he's soft and fleshy,
aim for him 'cause he'll forgive.

Your parents have gone out again
leaving you home alone,
now is the perfect time to play
a game called Fearless Chef.

The goal of this fantastic game
is to prepare a dish—
a dish so good it rivals all,
so here's the recipe:
Fill your dad's shiny work shoes
with your mom's best perfume,
then cover them from toe to heel
in frothy shaving cream.
Top with a mix of motor oil
and sticky black mascara,
then toss into the pot of soup
that your mom made for dinner.
Cover and simmer for a while
take care it doesn't burn.
You'll see how this dish turns out
when Mom and Dad return.

Washing hands and knees and toes
is a waste of children's time.
Never do it. It is stupid.
Absolutely pointless too!
Children's hands and knees and toes
will promptly dirtify again.
So why waste your time and effort
doing silly things like that?
Yet another worthless chore
is a haircut just because
by the time you're old and ancient
you'll be bald no matter what.

When your mom insists on dragging
you to see the dentist
don't count on any sympathy,
don't waste your tears on her.
No, be silent with conviction
and clench your jaw shut tight
so no dentist can get in there
even with all his might.

Those who've not jumped off their roof
holding only an umbrella,
cannot call themselves a daring
nor courageous Parachutist.
They'll never get to fly above
the worried crowds who've amassed.
They'll never get to lie in bed
with their leg in a cast.

Remember kids, if you are lost,
someone will bring you home
the minute that you give them
your exact house address.
So, use your head and say instead:
that you live with a monkey
on a remote and sandy beach
beneath a swaying palm tree.
So, if you happen to be lost
and you're not a dummy,
you shouldn't miss the opportunity
to see a foreign country!

MIKHAIL YASNOV (1946–2020) was a poet, translator, editor, and activist. Yasnov was born in Leningrad, and later graduated from Leningrad State University's Department of Philology. In the late 1970s, he published several books of translations from French and his own original children's poetry. As a translator, Yasnov was best known for his translations of Guillaume Apollinaire, Arthur Rimbaud, Paul Verlaine, and Charles Baudelaire; he also translated children's texts written by Maurice Carême, Vercors, and Pierre Gripari. Yasnov authored several poetic collections for children, the first of which, *The Yawning Medicine,* came out in 1979. Since that time, Yasnov wrote approximately a hundred books for children and published more than a hundred translations. Yasnov's first book of lyric poetry came out in 1986; by 2016, he had published eight more. In 2014, Yasnov published a collection of essays and articles on children's poetry titled *A Journey to Wonderhood: A Book about Children, Children's Poetry, and Children's Poets.* Yasnov was actively involved in children's radio, workshops for children and emerging writers, and competitions for children and young poets. Yasnov received multiple Russian and international awards for his poetry and translations, including the 2009 Chukovsky Prize, the 2012 Russian Federation Government Prize, and the 2014 Marshak Prize. Yasnov's poems "Kitty-cat and Ratty-rat" (1991), "Us and Birds" (1994), "Autumn Grandpa" (1999), and "A Little Tree with Wings" (2003) first appeared in poetry collections for children.

Kitty-cat and Ratty-rat

Translated by Ainsley Morse

On a fine cloudless morning,
With June just up to bat,
On a wide sunny porch
Lay the sweet Kitty-cat.
Yawning and licking her paws,
She admired her claws.
Then right past the Kitty-cat
Swiftly ran the Ratty-rat.
And the Ratty-rat said:
"What terrible manners!
Tell me, if you please,
Who on earth dares
To yawn with such ease?
It is time you, my dear,
Call to mind,
You must cover your mouth
With a paw—that's refined!
And what's more,
It's a scandalous habit, I say—
Licking your paws
All the livelong day.
It is time you, my dear,
Call to mind:
Paws are covered in germs
And cannot be licked—front or hind!
And what's more,
Your posture is making me sick,
My dear girl—
There's no pride in your pose,
Sweet puss—not a lick.
It is time you, my dear,
Save some face:
When out of doors one must
Lie around with grace!"

On a fine cloudless morning,
With June just up to bat,
On a wide sunny porch
Lay the sweet Kitty-cat.
Yawning and licking her paws,
She adjusted her jaws . . .
Deep down in the Kitty-cat
The Ratty-rat said naught . . .

Us and Birds

Translated by Ainsley Morse

We're going over birds at school,
Everything there is to know—
How they're built and feathered,
What they eat and how they grow,
How they fly and soar.
We're going over birds at school.
But they—
They're going over top of us,
Looking at the classroom lights
And they could care 'bout us.
They live up there in branches thick,
Raising up their young'uns,
While we schoolkids scribble on,
Raising hell in classrooms.
But what if it was opposite—
If we were flying free,
Then they'd be going over us
All year at school—sorry!
What we talk about and cram,
Who ate what while out at recess,
Who picked fights and who got slammed . . .
While we would just go fluttering round
And sing them songs, I guess!

Autumn Grandpa

Translated by Ainsley Morse

The wind has squashed the clouds together
And gotten quite exhausted.
The ancient rain goes plop and plop
And shuffles round the garden beds.
The garden, like a baby, quiets down,
And there amid the starts and straw,
In his slippers, dressing gown,
Wanders Autumn Grandpa.
He has also gotten soaked—
Like the greens and beds,
But he makes sure that everyone
Has a place to rest their heads.
And out he looks from wet and dark,
And taps upon the windowpane:
Everyone at home asleep?
Are we asleep?
I am.
I dream of rain.

A Little Tree with Wings

Translated by Ainsley Morse

I found a dead bird
Beneath a small tree—
I covered it up at first
With fallen leaves,
But afterward
I thought some:
What if someone's cat
Tries to have a little fun?
So I dug a big deep hole
Like for a treasure chest—
A cozy hole,

A soft one,
Like a little nest,
And made a little mound
Of dirt with my palm,
And again
I thought some.
What if,
I thought,
This time next year,
Like a seed,
My bird will sprout,
Peck its way out,
See the sun—
And a little tree with wings
Starts growing?
Then I watered
My little mound
And stuck in a stick at the top,
So in the spring
I'd find the spot,
Not wander confused all about . . .
Oh birdie, please,
Peck your way out!

SERGEI SEDOV (b. 1954) was born in Moscow. He is a children's writer who first worked as a teacher, an art model, and a yard-keeper. Sedov began publishing his short stories and tales in 1988 in the children's magazines *Cucumber, Murzilka,* and *Streetcar*. Along with other well-known children's poets and writers of the time, Sedov was a part of an influential literary collective, The Black Hen, which published its manifesto in *Pioneer* magazine in 1990. In the manifesto, the group proclaimed it was time to abolish the didactic and moralistic tone pervading Soviet children's literature. Sedov has published multiple collections, including *Zmei Gorynych's Tales* (1993), *Heracles' 12 Great Labours: Reports from the Field as They Really Happened!* (2000, English trans. 2014), *Tales about Vova, Presidents, and Magic* (2007), and *Tales about Kings* (2008). Sedov's controversial and highly original *Tales about Moms* (2005) consists of short, humorous, and sometimes dark stories about mothers of all kinds: absentminded, fierce, wicked, drunk, loving, shopaholic, and even extraterrestrial. For the "Jewish Children's Book" project, Sedov, along with the scholar Menachem Yaglom, adapted the Talmud for children (2005). The selection of short stories below is from Sedov's most popular collection *Tales about a Boy Named Alex* (1991), about a boy who can turn into anything or anyone he wants: a bird, an airplane, a bear, or a truck.

Tales about a Boy Named Alex [excerpts]

Translated by Jamie Olson

Once upon a time there was a boy named Alex. He could turn himself into anything—anything at all! One time he turned himself into a pigeon, sat on the windowsill, and banged on the glass with his beak. His mama cried out, "Shoo! Why'd you land here?" She didn't recognize him, of course. So Alex said, "But I'm your son Alex, and you're my mama Lida!"

Then Mama understood everything and gave her son some seeds to peck at and some water to drink. Alex ate and drank his fill, and flew off to make different shapes in the air in front of the window. The neighbors looked on in wonder.

Then Mama said to them, "That pigeon is no stranger. It's my son, Alex! He's got exceptional abilities. I send him off to English classes, music lessons, and figure skating."

Alex and his mama went to the store. They bought all sorts of things: cabbage, potatoes, pineapples, bread, milk, two cakes, three watermelons, and four cantaloupes. It's one thing to buy stuff, but who's going to carry it all? Mama didn't have enough hands, and Alex was still too little.

All of a sudden, Mama saw a small truck parked nearby that looked a lot like Alex, and it nodded at her as if to say, let's go, Mama!

Mama sat down in the truck and drove away. But right then—a stoplight! A police officer blew a whistle and gave Mama a ticket because her truck had gone through a red light.

Back at home Alex's mama made her son stand in the corner and said, "I forbid you from turning into trucks or any other vehicles until you learn the rules of the road!"

Sometimes Alex liked to do nothing. Nothing at all. Entirely nothing!

One time he was sitting there doing nothing when his mama said to him, "Run down to the bakery. We haven't got any bread." But Alex didn't want to go. So, he went and turned himself into a loaf of bread and lay down on the table. He kept lying there, doing nothing at all. Meanwhile, Mama took out a big knife and got ready to slice a piece off! That loaf yelled so loud, jumped so quick, and ran so fast to the bakery . . . He was so scared he even forgot to turn himself back into a boy.

Alex turned into a vacuum cleaner, swallowed up all the dust, and then got tired of being a vacuum cleaner. He became a teapot. Mama even brewed tea inside him and set out some tasty jam on the table . . . Alex got envious of Mama and became—another mama.

So there were two mamas sitting at the table, drinking tea and talking about children. Alex's mama couldn't praise Alex enough: he so kind, and capable, and better than anyone! And the other mama, the fake one, nodded her head:

"Yes, yes, he's an exceptional boy. You should get him a dog, a huge one, and some cakes, twenty of them—no, thirty—and you should let him travel around the world in a hot air balloon too!"

Then the real mama understood who was sitting in front of her, saying such stupid things. And she didn't praise him anymore.

Once, a young teacher came to work at Alex's school. And she had her first lesson in Alex's classroom. But the kids saw that the teacher was young and inexperienced, so they started to make noise, shout, and break all sorts of rules. The teacher got flustered and didn't know what to do. But Alex liked her a lot. So he changed himself into the school principal and sat there, looking sternly from side to side. All of his classmates were afraid of the principal, so they immediately quieted down and began to listen carefully to the young teacher . . .

After a little while, the real principal of the school opened the door and peeked in at Alex's class. He wanted to see how the new teacher was handling discipline in the classroom. Then he saw himself sitting at Alex's desk.

"Oh," he said, "I'm already here! Well, in that case I don't need to worry about discipline."

Alex liked a certain girl who was really pretty. So pretty! He came up to her and said, "Let's be friends!" And they went for a walk in the yard. They walked and walked, but it was hot out, so the girl sighed, "Oh, what I would give for some ice cream right now!"

When he heard those words, of course, Alex turned immediately into an ice cream bar on a stick. And the girl ate him. She didn't even notice that Alex was gone. She threw away the stick and went to a dance. Then the stick turned back into sad Alex, sighed, and went home to his mama.

Alex didn't like that girl anymore. He liked a different one . . .

One time, Alex turned into a tiger and set off down the street. But everybody ran away from him in all directions, screaming, "Tiger!!! Tiger!!!" Only one young mother, with a stroller, didn't run away, because it's hard to run away from a tiger with a stroller.

But the tiger came closer and closer to the young mother. "Don't be afraid of me!" he said.

But the mother was afraid anyway. She shook with fear and said to the tiger, "Please don't touch my son, all right?"

"What are you talking about?" said the tiger, offended. "I'm not some kind of man-eater! I'm Alex. And what's your little boy's name?"

"My son's name is Vasily. So, you won't bite him?"

"You're so clueless!" the tiger roared. "I told you, but you won't listen. Well, then, watch!" And the tiger turned back into Alex.

The young mother hugged him, kissed him, and said, "I'm so happy that you're not a tiger!"

"Well," said Alex, shrugging, "what did I tell you?"

Then there was the time Alex turned into a birch tree. He stood there, rustling his leaves. And some dumb tourist looked at Alex and said, "What a nice birch! I should chop it down." And he took a swing at Alex with an axe.

But Alex grabbed him by the collar with a branch, lifted him into the air, pulled his pants down, and started to teach him a thing or two with one of his skinny little branches. He kept on smacking him and saying:

"Don't cut birches! . . . Don't cut firs! . . . Don't cut oaks! . . . Don't cut pines! . . . Don't cut apple trees! . . . Don't cut cherry trees! . . . Don't cut ash trees! . . . Don't cut rowan trees! . . . Don't cut baobabs! . . ."

Alex knew the names of so-o-o-o-o many trees.

Once, Alex and his mama went into the forest to hunt for mushrooms. An hour passed, two hours—but they didn't find any mushrooms, not a single one. Mama became sad and bored, and she trudged along, sighing. "What a hard life I've got!" she thought. Suddenly, she saw a magnificent aspen bolete standing in a clearing—slim, tall, and beautiful. Mama was delighted; she cut off the mushroom and laid it in her basket. But the mushroom, of course, wasn't real. It was Alex. He climbed out of the basket and turned into a porcini. And such a gorgeous one! Sturdy, stout, and without a single worm. Mama saw him right away, admired him . . . and put him in her basket. She walked a little more, looking around, and pretty soon she found another porcini! Mama cheered up and kept walking, singing a song as she went.

"What a nice life I've got!" she thought. All told, she had found ten aspen boletes, twenty porcinis, and thirty chanterelles—her favorite.

But when they came out of the woods and Mama looked into her basket, there was nothing there.

Then Alex confessed everything to her. He thought she would start to scold him, but instead Mama hugged Alex, kissed him, and said, "Thank you so much for indulging me!"

There was no way Mama was going to get Alex a dog. One time, Alex himself turned into a poodle of exceptional beauty and ran along next to Mama. Everyone who came by admired him and envied Mama, asking her, where did you get such an exquisite poodle?

But then an enormous St. Bernard came out of the alley, and everyone started to look at him instead. So Alex turned into a St. Bernard too, but twice as huge! Then everyone started to envy Mama again, and someone said that if she took a dog like that to a dog show, he would definitely get a big gold medal, because he's clearly a winner. But Mama knew that a dog show was neither here nor there. She didn't take Alex to a dog show but gave him a big medal herself—only not gold, but chocolate, since he's the best of all.

One time, something happened at work that really upset Alex's mama.

Her boss shouted at her, saying that she was careless and didn't do her job well . . . But actually it was the boss who was a bad worker, while Mama was a good one.

Mama came home all in tears and complained to her only son Alex about her fate.

And then Alex decided to teach Mama's boss a lesson.

He turned into the boss who was in charge of that boss, the bad one, and called him into his office.

Oh, how he shouted at him! He slammed his fist on the table, stomped his feet, and threatened to fire him immediately.

That poor crummy boss, he stood there, stiff as a board, wiped the sweat from his brow, and muttered in confusion, "What for? . . . What for?"

"For yelling at my mama!" answered Alex honestly.

"I won't do it again!" cried the boss. "Just tell me who your mama is, since there are a lot of different mothers who work for me."

But Alex wouldn't tell him. So the bad boss never learned which mother he shouldn't shout at. Ever since then, he doesn't shout at moms at all. Only at dads.

ANDREI USACHEV (b. 1958) has been writing prose, poetry, nonfiction, and educational books for children since 1985. Born in Moscow, Usachev graduated from the Department of Philology at Tver State University, after which he worked as a drummer in an orchestra, a dishwasher, a watchman, and a beach cleaner. He later became an editor for the magazine *Merry Pictures*, and a founder of the first independent children's magazine, *Streetcar* (1987–1988). He has published dozens of collections of poetry and fairy tales, and alphabet books and textbooks for young children in math, biology, geography, history, and art history. In *Adventures of a Little Person* (1994), Usachev retells the "Universal Declaration of Human Rights." Usachev and Eduard Uspensky published a volume of children's horror stories titled *Terrifying Children's Folklore* (1998). Usachev has written and performed songs for children, authored children's plays and screenplays for animated films, and served as the anchor of several TV and radio programs for children. Usachev has received many literary prizes, including the 2007 Marshak Prize, the 2009 Chukovsky Prize, and an honorable mention for the Hans Christian Andersen Prize (2012). The selected stories in this volume are from the collection *Smart Dog Sonya* (1996), one of Usachev's most popular books.

Smart Dog Sonya [excerpts]

Translated by Jane Bugaeva

King's Pooch

In a certain city, on a certain street, in a certain building, in apartment #66 there once lived a small, but very smart dog named Sonya.

Sonya had black, twinkling eyes and long eyelashes like a princess. She also had a trim little tail that she fanned herself with.

She also had an owner whose name was Ivan Ivanovich King. That's why their poet neighbor nicknamed Sonya a "king's pooch." But all the other neighbors thought that was her breed. And Sonya thought so too. And so did all the other dogs. And even Ivan Ivanovich King thought so! Even though he knew his last name better than anyone.

Every day Ivan Ivanovich went to work and Sonya was left alone in her king's apartment where she was very bored. That's probably why all sorts of interesting things happened to her. After all, whenever you're very bored, you want to do something interesting. And when you want to do something interesting, something interesting will surely happen. And when something interesting happens, you start to think: how did that happen? And when you start thinking, for some reason you become smarter. But why that is—no one knows.

And that's why Sonya was such a smart dog.

Puddle

Back when Sonya wasn't yet a smart dog, but only a smart puppy, she often peed in the hall.

Her owner, Ivan Ivanovich, would get very angry and rub her nose in the resulting puddle and say, "Who is responsible for this puddle? Who? Good dogs wait to be let outside and do not make puddles in the house!"

Naturally, Sonya hated being scolded. But instead of waiting, she tried to do her business discreetly on the rug—because she never left any puddles there.

Then one time, when they had gone out for a walk, Sonya saw a giant puddle in front of their building.

"Who could be responsible for such a giant puddle?" wondered Sonya. Next to it she saw another puddle, even bigger than the first. And then a third one . . .

"It was probably an elephant!" concluded Sonya. "He must've waited for a very long time," she thought with respect.

From that day on, Sonya stopped peeing in the apartment.

Hello, Thank You, Goodbye!

One day, an elderly Dachshund stopped Sonya in the stairwell.

"Well-mannered dogs always greet one another," said the Dachshund sternly. "That means they say, 'hello', 'hi', or 'good day' and wag their tail."

"Hello," said Sonya, who obviously wanted to be well-mannered. She gave a quick wag of her tail and went on her way. But before she had reached the Dachshund's middle—the dog turned out to be remarkably long—she heard again:

"Well-mannered dogs are polite," said the Dachshund. "If they are given a bone, a treat, or some good advice, they say 'thank you!'"

"Thank you!" said Sonya, who obviously wanted to be well-mannered and polite, and kept going. But just as she'd reached the Dachshund's tail, she heard behind her:

"Well-mannered dogs have common courtesy and always say 'goodbye' when departing."

"Goodbye!" yipped Sonya—satisfied that she was now a well-mannered, polite dog with common courtesy—and ran after her owner.

From that day on, Sonya was always very polite. Any time she passed a dog she'd say, "Hello, thank you, goodbye!"

What a shame that she mostly came across dogs of ordinary length, who were long gone by the time she'd finished.

How Sonya Learned about Electricity

One day, Sonya was watching her favorite TV show *In the World of Animals*, and got to thinking, "How come people can talk but animals can't?"

Then it dawned on her! "The TV talks when it's plugged into a power outlet…" she thought. "Which means, if I'm plugged into an outlet—I'll talk too!"

So Sonya went and stuck her tail into a power outlet. To her surprise, someone bit her from inside.

"Ow, ow, ow!" yelped Sonya. "Let go! It hurts!" She yanked out her tail and jumped away from the outlet.

Her astonished owner ran in from the kitchen. "Oh my!" he said petting the shaking Sonya. "Silly pup, there's electricity in there. Be careful!"

"Electricity? I wonder what he's like?" thought Sonya, cautiously eyeing the outlet. "So small but so feisty . . . he needs to be tamed!"

She brought over a bone from the kitchen and put it in front of the outlet.

"Maybe he doesn't like bones? Or he doesn't want to be seen?" thought Sonya.

She put a chocolate candy next to the bone and went outside for a walk. But when she returned everything remained untouched.

"That so-called Electricity doesn't like delicious bones! And he doesn't like chocolate candy! How strange!" thought Sonya.

From that day on, she decided to stay away from power outlets.

The Stain

One day, Sonya was eating cherry jam right out of the jar and dripped some on the clean white tablecloth.

"Oh no!" cried Sonya. Her owner hated stains and always got very upset when Sonya climbed on the table with dirty paws or jumped up on his clean khakis.

"Now what?" thought Sonya, looking at the bright cherry stain.

She tried licking it off, but the stain didn't lick off—quite the opposite, for some reason it only grew bigger.

Sonya started to lick some more: she licked and licked and licked . . . but the more she licked the bigger the stain grew! And soon the neat little drop of jam turned into a huge red stain the size of a plate . . .

"Before long, the stain will be as big as the whole tablecloth!" thought Sonya hopelessly.

But then she had a brilliant idea! Sonya poured what was left of the jam onto the table and began spreading it all around.

"No more cherry stain! Now, it'll be a beautiful cherry tablecloth!" thought Sonya as she smeared and licked the jam all over the tablecloth.

When she'd finished, Sonya proudly admired her handiwork, but then with horror she noticed the jam jar—it had left a bright white spot on the beautiful cherry tablecloth! Sonya peeked inside the jar, but there wasn't even a drop of jam left.

Oh, how Ivan Ivanovich scolded her when he saw the spot—even though it was perfectly clean and white.

"Just imagine what would've happened," thought Sonya, "if I would've left that messy, red stain—I get shivers just thinking about it!"

How Sonya Lost Everything

One day Ivan Ivanovich went into a store and told Sonya to wait for him outside. Sonya sat and sat, waited and waited, when she suddenly had a thought, "Why am I waiting for him here? Since he went in through the entrance, he'll surely come out of the exit." And she ran to the exit.

She sat and sat, waited and waited—but her owner didn't come out.

"Then again," thought Sonya, "why would he leave through the exit when he left me by the entrance?" And she ran back to the entrance.

But Ivan Ivanovich wasn't at the entrance.

"Strange," thought Sonya. "I bet when he didn't find me, he went back into the store!" And she ran into the store. She sniffed up and down all the aisles and barked up and down all the people waiting in line, but she didn't find Ivan Ivanovich.

"I know!" said Sonya. "While I was looking for him here, I bet he was looking for me at the exit."

But there was no one at the exit.

"Oh no!" though Sonya. "I think Ivan Ivanovich is lost!"

She desperately looked around and suddenly saw a sign that said "Lost and Found."

"Excuse me," she addressed the old woman behind the counter. "I've lost my owner."

"People don't bring owners here," she said. "Bags or watches—now that's another story. You haven't lost a watch, have you?"

"No," said Sonya. "I don't wear one."

"Too bad," said the old woman. "If you wore a watch and had lost it, we would have definitely found it. As for your lost owner—go the police."

Sonya left the "Lost and Found" very upset but immediately saw a police officer. He was standing in the middle of an intersection blowing his whistle shrilly.

"Woof woof, Officer," said Sonya. "I've lost my owner."

The police officer was so surprised that he stopped blowing his whistle.

"Name, patronymic, and last name of the lost person?" he asked, getting out a notebook.

"Ivan Ivanovich . . ." after that Sonya was at a loss. "I've never asked his last name."

"That's not good," said the officer. "Do you know where he lives?"

"Yes!" said Sonya happily. "We live . . ."

That's when Sonya realized that along with her owner she had lost everything: her apartment, her apartment building, her street . . . and everything else!

"I don't know . . ." she said, almost crying. "What should I do?"

"Put an ad in the evening newspaper," suggested the officer, and he showed Sonya where the newspaper press was.

"What have you lost?" asked the person behind the window labeled "Lost" (next to it where three other windows: "Found," "For Sale," and "Looking to Buy").

"Everything," said Sonya. "Please write: little dog Sonya has lost her owner, Ivan Ivanovich, along with a lovely one-bedroom apartment, a twelve-story brick building, an inviting yard with a flowerbed, a playground, a trash can, and a fence under which is buried . . . actually don't write that last part, who knows what people might think!" said Sonya. "As well as a big street with a grocery store, an ice cream stand, the streetcleaner Sedov . . ."

"Enough," said the person behind the window. "All that won't fit."

In the end the newspaper only had enough room for a very short ad:

"Lost dog: Sonya. Reward if found."

That evening Ivan Ivanovich ran to the newspaper press.

"Who gets the reward?" he asked looking all around.

"Me!" said Sonya smiling bashfully. And at home she got a whole jar of cherry jam.

Sonya was very happy and even thought about getting lost again sometime . . . But she made sure to memorize her owner's last name and address. Because without knowing that, she really could lose everything!

LUDMILLA PETRUSHEVSKAYA (b. 1938), a writer, poet, playwright, and performer, was born in Moscow and graduated from Moscow State University with a degree in journalism. Petrushevskaya co-authored the script for Yury Norshtein's renowned animated film *Tale of Tales* (1979). Most of her dark and grotesque works are written for adults, including the novels *The Time: Night* (1992) and *The Number One* (2004). The collection *There Once Lived a Woman Who Tried to Kill Her Neighbor's Baby,* which includes short stories written in the 1990s, was published in the United States in 2009 and received the World Fantasy Award. Petrushevskaya's memoir-like *The Girl from the Metropol Hotel* was published in Russian in 2006 and in English in 2017. She has written fairy tales both for adults and for children. Petrushevskaya has received multiple awards, including the Russian Federation State Prize (2004). *Piglet Peter Drives a Car* and *Piglet Peter at the Store* are two of three picture books for very small children that Petrushevskaya created with illustrator **Alexander Reichshtein** (b. 1957) in 2002. A song with a subversive political subtext by internet user "Lein" made Piglet Peter a popular Russian meme. Later Petrushevskaya and Reichshtein published several other stories about Piglet Peter with the title *Piglet Peter: New Adventures* (2020).

Ludmilla Petrushevskaya, *Piglet Peter Drives a Car*, illus. Alexander Reichshtein (Moscow: OGI, 2002). Courtesy of Rosman Publishing House.

Piglet Peter Drives a Car

Translated by Jane Bugaeva

Once upon a time there lived a Piglet named Peter.

He decided to make himself a car.

So, he went to his room and sat on a chair—but he soon realized something was missing.

Peter went to the kitchen and asked his mama for a pot lid.

"Don't lose this," said his mama and gave him a lid.

Peter took the lid and went back to sit on his chair.

He held the lid in his hands and turned it this way and that.

"Vroom! Vroom! Beep beep!" he yelled, as all cars do.

Suddenly he was in a car, gripping the steering wheel.

And his car took off, driving down the street with Peter steering it along.

He was going very fast and passing everyone!

All the pedestrians—the chickens, cows, and other piglets—were quite surprised.

Piglet Peter at the Store

Translated by Jane Bugaeva

Puppy Marusya found a lot of rocks and decided to open up a candy store.

Piglet Peter came to her store.

"What's good here?" he asked.

"I'm selling candy," said Marusya.

It was true—her store was filled with lots of beautiful candy. She would weigh it on a scale and wrap it up in paper.

"I would like a lot of big candy," said Peter.

"OK. Pay me some money," said Marusya.

"Fine," said Peter and walked off. But he didn't stumble upon any money.

But he did see Kitten Sasha.

"Where can I find some money?" Peter asked.

"There, under the tree! We have so much of it! Don't take the yellow money, take the green money!" said Sasha.

So Peter gathered up a lot of green money and put it in his pocket.

And he and Sasha ran to Puppy Marusya's store and gave her all of the green money.

Marusya took the money and weighed out a lot of candy.

And then they all sat down to enjoy the candy with some tea.

ARTUR GIVARGIZOV (b. 1965) is one of the most popular contemporary children's poets, and a writer in the OBERIU tradition of funny, ironic, absurdist poetry for children. Born in Kyiv, Givargizov graduated from the Music School of the Moscow Tchaikovsky State Conservatory in 1989 with a specialization in guitar. Givargizov played in an orchestra and a medieval music group while also teaching guitar at a music school. His first selection of poetry and short stories was published in *Satirikon* magazine in 1997. Givargizov's first book, *My Poor Sharik,* came out in 2002. Since then, he has published several dozen books of poetry, short stories, and plays for children, among them *With the Wardrobe on the Bicycle* (2002), *We're So Alike* (2008), *King's Honor* (2011), *When There's No Time* (2012), and *Such Different Olyas* (2014). His latest books are *Necessary Dog* (2024), and *Not about Everything* (2024). In 2008, Givargizov became the founder and editor of the series Multicolor Square (Egmont Publishing House), committed to combining the best contemporary texts for children with the work of top illustrators. Givargizov has received many literary awards, including the 2003 and 2006 Scarlet Sails Prize and the 2011 Chukovsky Prize. Two of Givargizov's books were included in the Munich International Youth Library White Ravens List (2007 and 2012). The three stories in this volume are from the collection *Notes of a Distinguished F Student* (2005), and the poems are from Givargizov's *Generals* (2011).

Notes of a Distinguished F Student [excerpts]

Translated by Alexandra Berlina

The Faculty Meeting

One day, teachers invited Sergei Gavrilov—a distinguished F student and a veteran of the 4th grade—to the faculty meeting to give a talk entitled "Why children do not want to learn or do their homework."

"The sage acts by doing nothing. The sacral value of non-action is the law of the heavenly Tao," Sergei began. "When all learning is gone, there shall be no more sorrow." He sighed deeply.

"But what about physics?!" the physics teacher shouted from her seat. "Without physics, Gavrilov, you wouldn't even know that the Earth is round!"

"It is?" Sergei asked in surprise.

"You bet!" The geography teacher thrust her hand into her bag and triumphantly produced a cast-iron globe, which she always carried with her for self-defense. "That's how round it is!"

"All right," Sergei chuckled, pointing at the ocean, "then why doesn't all the water come off?"

"It's because the Earth attracts it! Like a magnet!" The physics teacher jumped up from her seat again, blushing with excitement.

"Magnets don't attract water," explained Sergei and closed his tired eyes. "I knew this back in kindergarten."

"So, Master Sergei," the school principal inquired politely, "you choose to believe that the scientists were all wrong, and all the sacrifices were in vain?"

"Errare humanum est," said Sergei, "to err is human. Cicero." He spread his hands. "I understand your consternation, and believe me, I am very sorry."

"Come again?" asked the history teacher. "I need to write it down. Errare humanum what?"

"Est," said Sergei.

A Missed Lesson

Myachikov took a running start and jumped.

"A meter forty," the gym teacher said, "Myachikov, you should really take up high jumping: you might become a champion."

Myachikov shrugged and set the bar at two meters and eighty centimeters.

"Stop fooling around," the gym teacher said, "this is higher than the world record."

Myachikov took a running start and jumped.

The gym teacher gasped and fainted.

"So now what's wrong?" asked Myachikov in surprise.

He leaped into the air and stayed there, floating.

"Gravity is supposed to pull you back," Serebertseva explained. She was an A student.

"Why?" asked Myachikov.

"Because we had it in physics last week," Serebertseva explained.

"I missed the lesson," said Myachikov. "I was ill. Got a doctor's notice and everything."

"Still, you were supposed to learn it," said Serebertseva.

"Okay, so gravity it is," Myachikov consented grudgingly, flopping onto the mat.

How Sergei Lost All Respect on September 9, in Gym Class

Sergei was very respected by his peers because he was the strongest. This was confirmed by his grade in gym class, which was always an A+.

Everyone went to Sergei for advice. For instance, how to deal with a school transcript if it has a F in it? And with the teacher who gave you that D? And with your parents if they just won't buy you a computer? And with that stuck-up Serebertseva?

Sergei was always happy to give free advice. For instance: to dissolve the school transcript in Pepsi, to put some pepper on the teacher's paper tissues and a cactus up his coat sleeve, to get back at the parents by getting the mumps on purpose, and as for Serebertseva, to give her a good shove, as usual.

By and by, Sergei got used to his position and stopped enjoying it. So he wrote "no free advice" on a piece of paper and hung it on his chest.

But Sergei's classmates just couldn't do without his advice! They sighed, they grumbled, and they paid. No one had any money, so they paid with their sandwiches.

Sergey ate and ate and ate and ate. After three months, he got so fat that he couldn't even get off the floor, let alone jump a meter twenty.

So, he started getting bad grades in gym class. No matter how much he yelled at the teacher "Hey, are you out of your mind?! It's me, Sergei!" she still gave him F's.

And then disaster struck—Zubov called Sergei a blimp. Sergei wanted to give him a good kick, but he just couldn't lift his leg.

From that time on, Sergei lost the respect of his peers, and of course no one turned to him for advice anymore.

Generals [select poems]

Translated by Alexandra Berlina

A General Divulging Military Secrets

A military secret can only be told to a fish.
Which is why the general takes up a fishing rod,
goes to a pond, catches a carp, whispers his secrets—
every new type of weapon, encryption, code—
lets the carp go, reels the line in, heads home, relieved.
Why does the general talk to an unknown carp?
What a question! The fishing helps with the tension.
Else his scalp starts itching under his cap.

A General Reviewing His Troops

The general is the tallest because he's on top of a horse.
Everyone else barely reaches up to his knee.
There he is, on the square, reviewing his force.
Not the Red Square, of course.
Rather, a square in the village of Maly Pni,
at his dacha. Nice place, though it takes a bit of commuting.
A fine, level ground, with concrete on top.
But the cows are no good at saluting.
Well then, some marching. Hoofs at the ready! Clop!

A General on an Island

One day, a general ended up on an island.
An island without a practice ground or any troops.
He'd never been so bored before in his life!

"Stand to attention, men!" he commanded. Oops,
there was no one to hear him. One, two, one:
there he marches, patrolling the island's border.
What does a general need for his heart's content?
Easy: a field flag, a drum and, of course, an order.

DINA SABITOVA (b. 1969) is from Kazan, Tatarstan, where she taught at Kazan State University after earning her PhD in linguistics. She began writing fairy tales at the age of ten. After leaving her teaching position and moving to Moscow, Sabitova returned to writing; her stories have appeared in *Cucumber* magazine and on the Internet. Her first novel for children, *Circus in a Treasure Box,* received the Incredible Dream Prize in 2007. Sabitova has published two novels for adolescents, *No-Winter Land* (2011) and *Your Three Names* (2012). She has also written an illustrated book for younger children, *Glikeria the Mouse: Multicolor and Striped Days* (2011). In four of her five books, Sabitova's main protagonists are orphaned children. The parent of an adopted child, she wrote *Tales about Martha* (2011) for the project "To a New Family," in which she presents adoption in a positive light for very young children. In 2012, Sabitova was nominated for the international Astrid Lindgren Award. Several of Sabitova's books have been translated into French, Latvian, Spanish, and Ukrainian. In 2013, Sabitova moved to Costa Rica where she opened a small hotel. *Circus in a Treasure Box* (2008) is a fantastical fairy tale about an orphan named Marik, who runs away from his orphanage to join the circus, where he finds his true home.

Circus in a Treasure Box [excerpts]

Translated by Andrea Lanoux

Chapter 1. How the Carouselli Circus Lost Its Clown, and Adelaida the Horse Lost Her Éclair

Sleeping standing up isn't very comfortable. Even if you're a horse. And if you're a circus horse in the famous Carouselli Circus, then you have to adjust to all kinds of situations. As everyone knows, circus horses are the least finicky creatures on earth.

Truth be told, the Carouselli Circus isn't especially famous. It travels around to small towns in the kingdom, putting on two performances a day. Even at that rate, many months go by when they can't afford new costumes for the horses or more colorful playbills.

Adelaida the circus horse awoke to a ruckus coming from the director's van.

"I will not stay at this second-rate, farce of a circus a moment longer! I've been recruited to the best circus in the capital—with my own featured performance! As you know better than anyone, I've been working myself to the bone here because there's no one else to perform between acts!" shouted an angry voice from that direction.

Adelaida knew that Pe the clown was causing the ruckus. She also knew what a featured performance was. It was when everyone was sitting in the wings in their cages, waiting for the performers to finish their acts so that the cashier can give them the audience's money. Then the performers treat the entire troupe to tea and pastries, and each animal gets the treat they like best. Adelaida, for instance, likes éclairs. So, if Pe the clown were to leave the circus, then some other horse from the capital would get her éclair. How sad.

"Although," thought Adelaida shaking her head, "what else would you expect from a person with a name like that?" The world has so many people, dogs, and horses in it, not to mention parrots, monkeys, cats, sparrows, and various other small animals. With so little free space on earth, your name should be as long as possible so that it takes up the maximum amount of space on your behalf. For instance, Adelaida's full name is Adelaida Beatrice Violetta Hortensia Sweetie. She doesn't much like the last part, but nothing can be done about it since that is the name she is called most often. As in, "Get over here, Sweetie!"

Sometimes Adelaida doesn't respond, waiting for them to address her in a more polite fashion. As you recall, circus horses are not finicky creatures. So fine, let them call her Sweetie. But the name Pe is intolerably silly. Adelaida once again thought her favorite thought about long names; she considered herself to be very smart and reasonable. Just look at her head! Even the director's head is five times smaller than hers is. And he must have thought he was the smartest one in the entire circus.

Meanwhile, the door to the director's van flew open with an unpleasant thud: out hopped Pe the clown, all sweaty and red in the face. The director ran after him, wringing his hands and trying to say something in a high-pitched whisper so that no one could hear. He led Pe back through the door. The director didn't want the entire circus to know about the scandal. Everyone knew, however, that Pe had asked for a raise, and that the director had not given him one. What kind of raise could be given when, instead of better costumes, the horses received patches sewn together in an artistic way?

A half-hour later, everyone beginning with the director and continuing on down to the tiniest dog, Kitty, knew that Pe had packed up his things and left. He departed on foot, spitting goodbye in the direction of the director's van and kicking a stake that fastened the rope to the tent. The clown crossed the barren, trampled field covered with stunted brown grass, limping and dragging a heavy suitcase. Literally no one watched as Pe left the circus, for nobody at the circus liked Pe. Even Kitty, who liked watching spectacles of all kinds, turned away from the disappearing Pe and went to dig up the bone she had buried the previous Thursday.

Nobody liked Pe because of his repulsive personality. For one, he thought himself to be a great artist. For this reason, he felt his name should appear on the posters in big, red letters, and that everyone else's names should be small. And in gray. In fact, Pe felt deep down that no other names were needed.

Second, Pe was very greedy. He told himself, of course, that he was simply frugal. It was very unpleasant, however, when he would look into the animals' feeders and grumble that they were spending too much on food, when in his opinion their proceeds should be spent on the salaries of great artists. Even Kitty's little porcelain bowl irritated him, although its meager contents could hardly have increased the prosperity of a frugal clown.

Third, Pe had no sense of humor. You would think a clown without a sense of humor would be impossible, right? But Pe maintained that the main thing wasn't a clown's sense of humor, but his sense of calculation. He carried around a big notebook with a brown leather binding, the pages of which were covered with tables and numbers. Pe would calculate how many laughs he could expect per joke, the number of jokes per performance, and how many times he would have to shout "Oh-no-no!" in order to earn the salary he received from the director.

Pe's culminating joke was to go up to a bemused boy in the front row and grab him by the nose with two fingers. The boy would try not to cry, believing as he did that everything a clown did was funny, and all the happened at the circus was joyful. But his face would become downcast, and his nose would turn red. And then Pe would shout his famous "Oh-no-no!" and the audience would laugh. However, the boy would not return. And when there were no more boys in the town to come to the circus, the Carouselli Circus would move on.

Of course, Pe believed that his scientific approach to his work warranted extra pay. And today was precisely the day he decided to put this question to the director again. He had come with his notebook, in which he had carefully recorded all his jokes, every "Oh-no-no," and each of the boys he had grabbed by the nose. All of these things comprised the denominator, and the numerator was Pe's salary.

It turned out that although Pe was being compensated for tweaking the boys' noses, as well as for the jokes (although below market rate), he had been performing the "Oh-no-no's" at a loss. The director then reached for his own accounting books, from which it became abundantly clear that giving anyone a raise of any kind was simply not an option, since their earnings totaled just enough to cover their most pressing needs.

The end of the conversation is well known. The director sat on a little bench outside his van, holding his head in his hands and mumbling in a piteous tone. From time to time he would raise his head and glance around, his eyes full of sorrow.

He saw that things were how they always were.

Rio Rita, the stunt rider, was hanging her colorful, freshly washed tights on a clothesline between the vans, along with her curtains patterned with little blue flowers. Tiny Kitty was burying her bone for the third time in a new spot. Adelaida-Sweetie was chatting quietly with some of the other horses, nibbling dry grass at the edge of the brown, barren field. Fillip the donkey was loitering nearby, listening with great interest to the conversations of the actual horses.

Kitty's owner, Mademoiselle Kazimira, was sitting on the steps of her van drinking coffee with cream. Johannson the Magician had dragged his shiny table of mirrors into the sun and was hitting it with a hammer, humming something absentmindedly. During his last performance the table had nearly crushed him when the rabbits, having disappeared into the hat correctly without a trace, came climbing out. Only Pe's loud "Oh-no-no!" saved the act from being a total disaster.

The gymnasts Flick and Flack were rehearsing somewhere off to the side, as was Hop the juggler. Although they couldn't be seen, they could be heard: judging by the voices coming from their direction, Hop had hit one of the gymnasts in the head with a flyaway juggling club. Meanwhile, Melodius the Human Orchestra was making a glue to repair some torn sheet music. In short, the director saw the entire troupe of the Carouselli Circus going about their usual business. Except there was no clown.

The truth is, a circus should be able to get by if a given act is absent: it can manage without jugglers, magicians, acrobats, even without a director (this point occurred to the director often, although he still trembled at the thought). The only thing a circus cannot do without are animals and a clown.

The director had no idea how to extract himself from this terrible situation. He just looked around and muttered to himself, "Well, now . . . isn't this a mess." And as evening approached and the closer it got to show time, the director's sighs became louder and more morose.

Chapter 8. How Marik Nearly Met His End but Was Saved

You know the details of how to ride a horse, don't you?

People wearing pants climb onto the horse's back, hug the horse's sides with their knees, and put their feet into the stirrups.

Ladies, however, ride horses in a very different way. Even if you don't have a horse, you can tell a real lady from a regular person by her umbrella: in the summertime, a real lady will undoubtedly be holding a lace umbrella, and she will have a bunch of frills and bows on her dress. But if you have a horse, you can tell a real lady by her unique way of riding it. If you suggest that she take a ride, she will undoubtedly say that she needs her riding habit (which is an extremely uncomfortable dress that ladies wear while riding horses). And once she dons her riding habit, she won't straddle the horse, but sit with her legs hanging off to the side. And to do this she will need a special side saddle, and she will undoubtedly try to hold her lace umbrella in one hand.

Adelaida the horse was familiar with the ways of lady riders. During her long life she had had more than one occasion to work with them. With a lady sitting on your back, you have to move slowly and carefully and watch your footwork. God forbid she fall off her side saddle and end up under your hooves—you'll never recover from the scandal.

But there is yet a third way to ride a horse. Circus style. That's how Rio Rita rides. If you were to meet Rio Rita in a city park, you wouldn't be able to tell her apart from a real lady. She has the lace umbrella and the dress with the bows—all of the accoutrements. But when she mounts a horse, you can tell right away that she is no lady, but a bona fide circus rider. Rio Rita can ride a horse upside down, standing on her hands, or—most spectacularly—doing somersaults in the air and landing perfectly on Adelaida's back. No lady in the world can do anything like that.

And if Rio Rita falls off a horse (which happens very rarely, almost never) she doesn't fuss like ladies do by asking for a hand to get up or require smelling salts in order to her come to her senses. And she doesn't say, "Oh, what a terrible horse, now my riding habit is a mess!" She simply gets up, runs after the horse, and continues practicing.

Adelaida is usually not to blame when Rio Rita falls; still, a horse feels somewhat embarrassed when this happens. She would like to say an encouraging word to the rider, although she knows it's better not to. Rio Rita would likely just laugh sarcastically and wave it off, as if to say "I don't need your sympathy, let's get back to work." That said, Rio Rita almost never falls.

But today when Rio Rita decided to warm up at a rest stop, something very unpleasant happened. A pebble rolled under Adelaida's hoof (maybe it was a piece of a root, no one could tell). The horse stumbled, and Rio Rita tumbled to the ground. She quickly jumped up, but then she gasped softly and stopped.

"What's wrong?" said Adelaida, running over with worry and a sense of guilt. "Did you sprain your ankle?"

"No, I think I hurt my arm," said Rio Rita, raising her right arm awkwardly and gingerly cradling her elbow with her left hand.

Mademoiselle Kazimira made it over to them, having watched the unfortunate event from afar. If it were something very serious, they would of course call a doctor, but when it came to setting dislocated limbs, dressing wounds, or curing colds, Kazimira did a fabulous job of taking care of such things herself.

"It's not too bad," she breathed a sigh of relief, examining Rio Rita's arm. "A bruise and a mild sprain. We'll apply a cold compress and bandage it up. You shouldn't use the arm for two or three days, though."

That's how it came to be that Rio Rita was unable to do dishes after lunch on that particular day, and why Marik had volunteered to do them himself. Mademoiselle Kazimira had offered to help, but Marik wanted to show that he could manage by himself.

He gathered all the plates and cups in a large basket and pulled them to the stream at the edge of the grove. It took him half an hour to wash the dishes;

when the last cup was clean, Marik decided to jump in himself. The day was hot, and laboring over the dishes had made him grimy and tired.

Throwing off his clothes, Marik ventured deep into the water, whooping under his breath in the frigid water, which now seemed colder than it had while he was splashing by the shore. Out here the water was darker, but you could still see the bottom clearly: the sand and pebbles swirled in the water and the tiny fish were as small as your pinky, rushing back and forth in a gray cloud and tickling Marik between his toes.

Marik closed his eyes, slapping the surface of the water with his palms and spinning around in place. He didn't know how to swim, so he shifted his weight from side to side on the hard, sandy bottom, turning his face to the sun: the light was rose-colored shining through his nearly closed eyelids; the tighter he closed them, the darker the color became . . .

Marik did not fully comprehend what happened next. The rosy light turned greenish, the bottom dropped out from under his feet, and Marik suddenly found himself underwater. He instinctively thrashed his arms and legs in a panic, broke through to the surface and shouted, floundering and trying to touch bottom. But there was no bottom. Cold water entered his mouth, nose, and ears: he couldn't breathe, and again he found himself under water. In short, Marik was drowning. The more he struggled to save himself, the faster he lost his strength.

Then, at that terrible moment, he felt a firm hand suddenly grab him and lift his head above the water, then drag him to the shore.

A few seconds later, Marik was lying on the sand, shaking from the cold and from the terrible scare he had just endured, spitting and coughing out water.

"You're alive, you're fine. You don't need to keep spitting," he heard someone say above him in a low, playful voice.

Pushing himself up on all fours, he turned to look at his savior.

The savior was female. The person who had pulled him out of the river was looking back at him, her head tilted to the side. Then she laughed and said, "If you're done drowning for now, you can close your mouth. I can't stop you from staring at me with your mouth wide open, but you look like an absolute goofball. One not entirely worth saving."

Marik closed his mouth. He continued to stare, though—how could he not! He had never seen such a strange woman in his life.

He thought: one could even call her an old woman. Actually, no—old woman didn't fit, since he couldn't tell how old she was. And "little old lady" was even less fitting. The woman standing before him was not young, that was the only thing he could say for certain.

Never in his life had Marik seen such a... strange, older woman. Since Marik was kneeling on all fours and his savior was towering over him, it was only natural that he visually take her in from the ground up.

A pair of boots. Far from new, they were well-worn and of a whitish color. The right boot was tied with a red shoelace, and the left with a dark-blue silk ribbon with shiny silver beads at the ends. Near the top of one of the boots someone had painted a little house.

Marik had never known anyone with hand-painted footwear. Before him was a painting of a neat little house with a tiled roof, a terrace, a balcony, tiny flower boxes along the terrace, and white steps leading down to the garden. The garden below had flowering lilac bushes, peonies, and apple trees. The painting continued onto the left boot where a tasseled barberry bush blossomed, and under the farthest bush there was a small watering can on which someone had drawn a...

Marik lifted his eyes. Above the painted boots with the little house were pants. Rather, a pair of overalls with wide shoulder straps. At first it seemed they were made of denim, but on second glance it was difficult to say.

It was hard to say because the pants, the front of the overalls, and the shoulder straps were all covered with one, two, three, four, ten (Marik lost count), maybe a hundred pockets: leather pockets, canvas pockets, velvet and silk pockets, pockets with buttons, snaps, zippers, or nothing at all. There were pockets on top of pockets, as well as single pockets. Some were wide enough to fit a book (it looked like there actually was a book in one), others were skinny as a pencil. Some of the pencil pockets had pencils sticking out of them, or something else altogether—a pocketknife, a silver spoon, a small flute, a telescope.

Over her right shoulder, a bright yellow and lilac striped rucksack appeared. On top of all of this splendor was a big, checkered hat with a flower.

"Are you done staring?" inquired the strange older woman. "So, what do you say?"

"Hello," Marik said. "Thank you for saving me."

"Hello. You're welcome," chuckled the not-quite-old woman. "It wasn't hard, it was a pleasure actually. What I don't like are boys who tell lies."

Marik was confused by the last part; forgetting all sense of decorum he blurted out, "Dang!"

"There we go. That's better," nodded his interlocutor. "I was afraid you were going to utter something like, "Forgive me, ma'am, I did not fully understand your concluding remark."

"I did not fully understand your concluding remark," Marik nodded, catching himself.

"You are obviously incorrigible. Maybe I shouldn't have pulled you out of the water with all of your dangs and deference. Maybe I should have let them drown . . ."

"Who, me?"

"No, your dangs and deference."

"Is it deferential to ask a dang question?" Marik asked playfully.

"Humm . . ." replied the not-quite-old woman. "It seems I've jumped to conclusions about you. You may have some potential after all."

"Why did you say that you don't like people who tell lies?"

"Because," sighed the not-quite-old woman, "what you were thinking was, 'Who in God's name is this person?' but instead you said 'thank you, ma'am,' etc."

Marik was taken aback at the direction the conversation was taking.

"Admit it," demanded the not-quite-old woman. "Who in God's name am I? You can get up off the ground—not because it's impolite, but it's just extremely uncomfortable to talk that way. What do you see?"

Marik sat on the sand. He clarified, "What should I do, tell you what you look like?"

"You don't have to do anything. But since I fished you out of the water along with your good manners, you should at least grant me a wish. So, tell me what thoughts were racing through your mind when you were sizing me up on all fours."

"I thought you looked like, I don't know . . . Miss Gertrude would probably say that you look like the village idiot."

"To hell with Miss Gertrude!" The not-quite-old woman shrugged her shoulders and continued. "I assure you that I'm much more normal than all the Gertrudes you've known, and have yet to know, in your lifetime. Not to mention, there are no villages around here, so the chances of my being a village idiot are next to nil."

"Well, in that case I would say that you look like . . . a clown."

"Magnificent!" his interlocutor nodded. "And now tell me, how did you end up in this brook?"

"From the circus," Marik sighed.

"So . . . do you mean to say that you came from the circus and promptly set about drowning?"

"First, I finished washing the dishes, then . . ."

"Wait," she interrupted, "you mean you are the only one at the circus who washes that enormous pile of dishes?"

"The thing is," Marik explained, "Rio Rita sprained her arm, and I wanted to show them how helpful I can be so that they don't send me back, because I really wanted to see the clown, but they don't have one anymore, and if they find him but they send me back I won't get to see him, and nobody knows where to find him . . ."

"Hold on a second, you're mixing it up. Tell me again from the beginning, in order."

"From the beginning would take a while." But he started again, and somehow, he managed to tell it in under four minutes. True, he left out the details about his life at the Little Apple Orphanage, saying only that "he lived in this one place, but then he left it."

Still, it seemed his new acquaintance was able to glean the main problem facing the Carouselli Circus. She nodded and said, "It's all clear to me now except for one thing: why is Rio Rita the only one who can do the dishes?"

"Because Mademoiselle Kazimira was busy, and . . ."

"I've heard about Kazimira. Besides those two, who else can do dishes?"

"They are the only women," Marik shrugged.

The not-quite-old woman scoffed: "Do the men—is it Hop? Flick? Flack? Johannson? Your Great and Terrible Director?—have hands made of marzipan that will melt if they touch dishwater? No. As soon as I become your clown, *everyone* will do dishes. I can assure you that it's considerably easier than juggling burning clubs or pulling rabbits out of a hat. I've done both, and dishes of course."

"When you become *what*?"

"A clown. Your clown. It appears I turned up on this shore just in time!"

MIKHAIL ESENOVSKY (b. 1960) was born in Moscow, where he currently lives. After obtaining a degree from Moscow State Technical University, he worked as a teacher and as a university lecturer. In 1991, Esenovsky became a member of a workshop for young writers led by Marina Moskvina and Marina Boroditskaya. He has worked as an editor of children's magazines and almanacs, and as a TV and radio children's programming anchor. Esenovsky's first book, *The Hospital,* was published in 1995, followed by *Hur-Yur-Gro,* a collection of short stories (2000). Esenovsky wrote several more books of poetry and prose, including *Where Are You, My Cabbage?* (2013), *The Moon behind the Couch* (2013), *The Fly from Malakhovka* (2016), and *Tasty Yura* (2018). Esenovsky's writing is zany and witty, and his sense of the absurd follows in the tradition of Daniil Kharms. Esenovsky's best-known book *The Essential Spy Question* (2009), with illustrations by **Natalia Korsunskaya** (b. 1976), received The Best Book of the Year for children's books at the Moscow International Book Fair. The main character, Yura, is a boy who is afraid of everything and everyone, and who also appears in other works by Esenovsky.

Mikhail Esenovsky, *The Essential Spy Question*, illus. Natalia Korsunskaya (Moscow: Izdatel'stvo Egmont, 2017). Courtesy of Natalia Korsunskaya.

The Essential Spy Question [excerpts]

Translated by Kelly Herold

There once was a boy named Yura who was very brave. He wasn't afraid of anything. Except for a few things.

For example, he was afraid of sleeping in his bed. This was because a crocodile slept under his bed sometimes. Yura lies in bed, but he's too scared to sleep.

"Crocodile," Yura said. "Are you there?"

"I'm here," said the Crocodile.

"But it's hard under the bed. And dusty," Yura said.

"It's fine," said the Crocodile. "The main thing is that you go to sleep, and quickly. The morning is wiser than the night!"

"Maybe I can put a cot in the hallway for you?" Yura asked. "It's drafty on the floor."

"Don't worry. I'm in great shape," the Crocodile said. "I take a cold shower every day."

"Excellent," Yura said. "And do you brush your teeth?"

"Of course, I brush my teeth. And I exercise every morning," the Crocodile said. "Any more questions?"

And Yura asked, "So, do you plan on eating me up with those very same teeth?"

"You are a weird human," the Crocodile said. "I have a wife at home. My little children cry—we have to have something to eat!"

"You're a parasite!" Yura said. "Maybe I want a wife and children? And you're going to eat me while I'm still a bachelor."

"Take it easy," answered the Crocodile. "By the way, I'm old enough to be *your* father."

"Sorry, *Dad*. I couldn't help it," Yura said.

"You see? No big deal. You are quite agreeable," said the Crocodile.

"Listen," Yura said. "One of my toy soldiers fell under the bed. Can you push it out with your tail?"

"So that's what's poking me in my belly!" said the Crocodile. "Here, take your soldier."

"Thanks," said Yura. "And maybe you can turn off my alarm clock?"

"No way," said the Crocodile. "You have to get up tomorrow morning, no matter what. Now go to bed."

The Crocodile stretched, yawned, and fell silent under the bed.

"Crocodile! Are you asleep?" asked Yura.

But the Crocodile was snoring his head off.

"Too bad," said Yura. "I just remembered a great joke. About crocodiles. I'll tell it to you tomorrow if I don't forget."

Besides the bed, Yura was afraid of all the dark rooms in his apartment. This was because a skeleton stood behind the curtains.

"Skeleton?" Yura called. "Are you here?"

The Skeleton was quiet. Only the curtains swayed gently.

"Skeleton," Yura said. "I am speaking to you. What, you don't hear me?"

"I'm here. What of it?" the Skeleton answered.

"Nothing," Yura said. "I was just wondering."

"Well, since you're here. Go to the window and look at that moon!"

"I get it," Yura said. "I'll go look at the moon, and you'll be waiting behind me to . . ."

"I do not need you at all!" said the Skeleton. "I said, go look at the moon."

Yura walked to the window and looked. It was true. There was a moon.

Yura pulled back the blinds. The Skeleton hadn't moved. Then Yura wrapped himself in the other side of the curtains and looked at the moon through the window.

"Skeleton, are there people on the moon?" he asked.

"No people," said the Skeleton. "Only skeletons live on the moon. Did you come just to ask stupid questions?"

"No, Mom sent me from the kitchen," Yura said. "She needs a towel."

"There's one hanging on the chair over there. Take it and go," said the Skeleton.

"What are you going to do?" asked Yura.

"I'm going to stand here a little. All sorts of thoughts are running through my skull."

"Okay. Then I'm off," Yura said. "Don't get bored here."

"What? I like to be alone," said the Skeleton.

"Alright, bye," said Yura.

"Will you come tomorrow?" the Skeleton asked. "There are still towels here in the closet. Maybe your mom will want them."

"I don't know. I have a lot of homework tomorrow."

"Okay. Study then," said the Skeleton. "If you need anything, I'm here. Just don't turn on the lights."

So Yura went to his mom in the kitchen and into the light. "Mom," he said. "What if we turn off the lights and drink tea, all of us together in the dark?"

Besides the dark rooms in the apartment, Yura was afraid of the laundry drying in the kitchen. Especially the sheet.

"Sheet," Yura said. "Please hang there quietly and stop fluttering. I came in here for some candy."

But the Sheet began fluttering wildly and said, "Maybe I want candy, too."

"I know what you want," said Yura. "I'll turn around and you'll strangle me. You only have one thing on your mind."

"You're so stingy! I have to choke people like you," said the Sheet.

"What? Did I make you mad?" asked Yura. "Go ahead, take the candy. I don't need it."

But the Sheet kept hanging and was silent.

"Okay, I'll leave it on the table," Yura said. "If you want it, take it."

When Yura arrived home from school, the candy was gone, and the sheet was all covered in chocolate.

"What a pig you are!" Yura exclaimed. "You could at least wash your hands! What will Mom say?"

Besides the laundry, Yura was afraid of Grandpa's portrait on the wall.

"Grandpa," said Yura. "Are you stuck there under the glass? Can't you come out?"

"It's all sealed up," said Grandpa. "You can't run away from out of here."

"That's good," said Yura. "Because you know, I'm afraid of you. Why do you always look at us so angrily?"

"I can't do anything about that," said Grandpa. "This is how they took my picture. Really, I was nice. You could even say jolly!"

"Did you love my Grandma a lot?" asked Yura.

"I couldn't have loved her more," answered Grandpa. "And I would have loved you too, if you had been born earlier."

"That's not my fault. It's all Mom and Dad's fault!" Yura said.

"Precisely," Grandpa said. "They took their time having you."

"They say I look like you," said Yura. "Are you glad that I do?"

"Absolutely. You go out in the world, and it's like I'm alive," said Grandpa.

"Grandpa, I'm still a little afraid of you," said Yura.

"Then be a little afraid," said Grandpa. "That's not bad. The main thing is not to forget me."

"I'll never forget you. If I go play with toy soldiers now, you won't be mad?"

"Go ahead," said Grandpa. "Just wipe the dust from the glass, please. Otherwise, I can't see well."

Besides the portrait, Yura was afraid of the walk-in closet, because in the closet, among the hangers and dresses, hid a Wardrobe.

"Wardrobe!" Yura said. "We're going to build a new walk-in closet soon, and then we're going to throw you in the trash, understand?"

"What will I do without you?" the Wardrobe asked from inside the closet. "I'm fully housebroken. I'd be lost on the outside."

"Maybe you're housebroken," Yura said to the Wardrobe. "Nevertheless, you have bad intentions."

"Bad intentions? I don't have any bad intentions!" the Wardrobe exclaimed. "Your mother's suits and striped pants just hang in here. What's your size, Yura?"

"I know what 'what's your size' means," Yura said. "I'll come close to you, and you'll pull me into the closet. It's scary to even think about what might happen."

"You don't mean that," said the Wardrobe. "I'm being sincere."

The Wardrobe took offence and fell silent. Just its door squeaked as if the Wardrobe was groaning sadly.

"Well, okay," said Yura. "Show me the pants then."

Yura tried on pants from the Wardrobe and hung his old pair in the closet.

"Now, that's much better," said the Wardrobe. "I'll clean and iron your old pants. Tomorrow they'll be just like new."

"The right pocket is ripped," said Yura.

"And maybe I should replace the zipper?" the Wardrobe asked. "I know how."

"Okay. I'll come see you after school," said Yura.

"We usually have lunch at 1:00," said the Wardrobe. "But drop on by, anyway. Say 'The skeleton sent me.'"

Yura closed the doors to the walk-in closet and went to his mother in the kitchen.

"Mom," Yura said. "You know, I'll just ruin a new walk-in closet with a penknife or something. Better use the money to buy yourself a fur coat and some kind of socks for Dad."

Besides the Wardrobe, Yura was afraid of the drain in the bathtub.

One time, Yura got into the bath, but he couldn't take his eyes of the Drain's hole. Yura sat further away and pushed water towards it in a wave.

The Drain spluttered and said, "Ouch! You pushed bubbles into my nose! Your shampoo is too sudsy."

"Then don't look at me! Why are you spying on me naked? Aren't you ashamed?"

"You don't think I've seen naked people before?" the Drain asked. "For some reason, everyone is naked here in the bathtub."

"Drain," said Yura. "Nothing will crawl out from you, will it?"

"Nothing," said the Drain. "I am empty and deep."

"Empty is good," said Yura. "But . . . deep is scary!"

"Don't be afraid. Why don't you stick your finger in me to see?" said the Drain.

"I'll put soap in you," Yura replied. "It has more vitamins."

"I don't want soap," said the Drain. "I like sucking on fingers."

"Yuck!" Yura exclaimed. "They're so dirty and microbes live under fingernails."

"So, wash them," the Drain said. "Why else did you get in the bath?"

Yura scrubbed his fingers with a washcloth and carefully stuck one finger into the Drain.

"Let's agree to not bite my fingernails," said Yura. "Or else, next time I'll smear mustard on them and then you'll see!"

The Drain sucked awhile on Yura's finger and said, "Now I want your pinkie. It's one of the sweetest fingers."

"Enough," said Yura. "I'm going to wash now, and you watch the faucet. It has a hole, too. Who knows what could happen!"

"Okay. You can count on me," said the Drain.

Yura washed peacefully and without trouble, and then he knocked on the wall and said to his Mom, "I want to get out now!"

"I guess you won't show up until Saturday now," said the Drain.

"Well, I might get dirty before then," Yura said.

Mom came into the bathroom, wrapped Yura up in a soft towel, and carried him to bed.

"Mom, do only robbers and bandits suck their thumbs?" Yura asked.

"Not only," Mom said. "Also, burglars and murderers!"

"That's okay," Yura said. "I can't only be friends with perfect people."

Besides the Drain, Yura was afraid of the front door. That was because a spy lurked behind the front door.

"Boy!" said the Spy behind the door. "What, let's say, is your name?"

Yura guessed this was the Spy speaking and answered, "My name is Yura."

He said this so that the Spy didn't guess that Yura had guessed, he was a Spy.

The Spy hadn't guessed about anything. He said, "Hey, Yura! When you grow up, will you be an astronaut?"

"What? Of course! I'll also be a janitor."

"A janitor? That's not very interesting," said the Spy. "Better be an astronaut. You'll grow up and tell me what's inside your rocket. I'll give you my phone number."

The Spy paused a moment for effect before asking the essential spy question. "Who do you love more—Mom or Dad?"

"I love them both equally," Yura answered. "The same. Uniformly."

"But surely you love one of them just a little bit more," said the Spy.

"It depends," Yura said. "Sometimes I like one of them more, then the other."

"But still, in the course of a year, you must prefer one of them?" said the Spy.

"Of course," Yura said. "But years are different."

"Well, okay," said the Spy. "But, in conclusion, after all your time with them, who would be in first place?"

"They would," said Yura. "As a pair. Together. And we decided not to bother with a third place."

"Whatever," said the Spy. "I'm tired of this."

The Spy took offense, removed the bulb from the landing light, and ran down the stairs skipping four steps at a time, nearly dislocating his foot.

NARINE ABGARYAN (b. 1971) is from the small Armenian town of Berd. She received her education at Yerevan Brusov State University of Languages and Social Sciences, before moving to Moscow in 1993, where she worked as an accountant and a salesperson. Abgaryan began her literary career as a blogger on the online platform LiveJournal, where she posted stories about the misbehavior and mishaps of a girl named Manyunya and her best friend Nara in a small Armenian town in the late Soviet period. These stories were collected into her blockbuster autobiographical novel for children *Manyunya* (2010). Two sequels followed in 2011 and 2012, and a ten-part television series was filmed in 2021. Abgaryan's books for adult readers include *Three Apples Fell from the Sky* (2015, published in English in 2020); the short story collections *Zulali* and *People of Our Yard* (both published in 2016); *To Go On Living* (2021, published in English in 2025); and the novel *Simon* (2020). Her children's book *Semion Andreich: The Scribble Chronicles* (2012) won the 2013 Baby-NOS Prize for the best children's book of the decade. The book's colorful and lighthearted illustrations are by Moscow artist **Victoria Kirdii** (b. 1966). The main character is a boy of five who is so thoughtful that his mom calls him by his name and patronymic, Semion Andreich, as if he were a grown-up. He is a happy kid: he celebrates his birthday, likes skiing in the park, falls in love, makes new friends, and spends time at a summer house. He has just learned how to write, but his spelling is still a problem.

Narine Abgaryan, *Semion Andreich: The Scribble Chronicles*, illus. Viktoria Kirdii (Moscow: Rech', 2012). Courtesy of Viktoria Kirdii.

Semion Andreich: The Scribble Chronicles **[excerpts]**

Translated by Cara Ehlenfeldt

Semion Andreich Celebrates a Birthday

Today Semion Andreich turned five. In honor of the occasion, Mama baked him a proper birthday cake and decorated it with strawberries and whipped cream. After that, she ran down to the sporting goods store and came back with a big pair of skis and a bicycle for Semion Andreich. Mama slyly hid the skis in the pantry.

"Mama probably got them for herself," Semion Andreich decided.

Mama's birthday is in a month, on February 16th. That's why she bought skis. And she hid them in the pantry, so she won't spoil the surprise for herself. A month from now, she'll rummage in the pantry and discover them. What a delight!

Semion Andreich was watching Mama's preparations from his room. If you cracked open the door a little bit, then every time she went past you could "just happen" to glimpse lots of interesting things. For example, how Mama tiptoed like a crane as she carried the skis. Mama always walks this way when she's trying not to make noise. But whenever you try not to make noise, the opposite happens. Therefore, she knocked the skis against everything in her path: the light fixture on the wall (*bzing!*), the kitchen door (*hrosh!*), the hall lamp (*ploom!*).

At each *bzing-hrosh-ploom* Mama cringed and told herself "Sh-sh-sh!" She said it so sternly, so painstakingly. But then she kept making noise: first she knocked over the bedside table with a crash, then she scraped the skis around in the pantry—she stood them up this way, then that way. To start, she simply leaned them against the wall, but the skis up and fell on her head. Next, she tried to slide them deep into the pantry, but the skis snagged on a box and pulled down a heap of old books. At long last, Mama thought to lean them diagonally from corner to corner, and the skis obediently stood still.

"Phew!" Mama puffed and went to wrap the bicycle with a blue ribbon.

Semion Andreich was sitting quietly in his room. He understands his mama very well. After all, he's lived with her for five years already. So he tries not to step on her toes when she's preparing a surprise. Mama especially doesn't like it when things get in the way of her gift-giving. She has just enough patience to bring in the present and wrap it. A minute longer, and her patience runs out, so she runs to deliver the gift to the birthday boy then and there. That's why she bought the bicycle precisely today and not yesterday or last week.

Fifteen minutes later, when she wheeled the present into her son's room—beautifully wrapped with a blue ribbon tied around it—there he was, sitting at the table, leafing through a book like a noble knight.

"Happy birthday to you, happy birthday to you, happy birthday, Semion Andre-e-e-ich, happy birthday to you!" Mama sang.

Semion Andreich ran to hug Mama first, then the bicycle. Then right away they started racing each other to tear off the crinkly paper and unwind the blue ribbon, and Mama looked like she had already forgotten what was under that beautiful wrapping. Afterwards Semion Andreich, cheerfully beep-beeping, rode from room to room, playfully braking and tracing out zigzags, while Mama set the table for his birthday celebration.

Soon Grandma and Grandpa from Strogino showed up to their grandson's party. Semion Andreich assumes that people struggle in Strogino. That's why it's called Strogino. Semion Andreich is extremely worried about Grandma and Grandpa. They are kind, smiley people, and how they survive in such a difficult place is a total mystery.

Grandma and Grandpa gave the birthday boy a big castle playset. Semion Andreich's happiness was boundless. He'd dreamed about this kind of playset for ages. Of course, he didn't go and open the box right away because he had to sit down at the table.

Grandpa poured sweet fizzy lemonade into their glasses and made a beautiful toast. Then Mama turned out the lights and brought in the cake with five burning candles. Semion Andreich made a wish and blew out all the candles in a single breath.

"Hooray!" Grandma clapped. "Our beloved Semion Andreich has turned five!"

"And what did you make when you blew out the candles?" Grandpa asked.

An uncomfortable silence set in.

"A want!" Semion Andreich sulked.

"What do you mean 'a want'?" Grandpa was dumbfounded. "You didn't make a wish?"

"I don't know," Semion Andreich shrugged and dragged the playset into his room.

"Pop, you forgot again!" Mama hissed reproachfully. "Wi*sh*! He can't pronounce the sound *sh*!"

"Goodness gracious!" Grandpa smacked himself in the forehead. "You aren't upset with me, are you?" he stuck his head into his grandson's room. "It's because of this blasted sclerosis that I keep forgetting about *sh*!"

Semion Andreich was putting together a big castle. He turned around toward Grandpa and smiled at him with his whole chubby-cheeked face.

"Grampa, there are even knights on horses here, with lances! And catapults! See?"

"Where?" Grandpa craned his neck. He clicked his tongue in admiration. Then he settled down beside his grandson, and he cheerfully assembled the playset with him the whole evening.

Semion Andreich went to bed late, at 11 o'clock. Since today was his birthday, he was allowed to stay up a little later. When Mama checked on him in his room—to tuck him in—Semion Andreich was asleep, curled up with his arm under his cheek. The toy castle, with its wide moat, drawbridges, pulleys, cannons, and catapults, was spread out on the floor. In the corner of the room, the headlight of his brand new bike gleamed. Semion Andreich's drawing book lay open on the table.

Mama glanced at it and read:

SKLEROZIS IZ A BLASTID DIZEEZ. IT NEEDZ TO BE KYURED.

Semion Andreich and the Sound sh

Twice a week, on Saturdays and Sundays, Mama takes Semion Andreich to see Alevtina Petrovna. Semion Andreich doesn't look forward to these visits. He resists in any way he can. He sprawls across the bed, rolls his eyes, and complains about having high blood pressure.

"You won't fool me with that trick." Mama dismisses all his feeble attempts. Semion Andreich sighs bitterly. While Mama helps him put on his warm winter coveralls, he lectures her on protecting the rights of five-year-old boys. It's not so awful that a certain boy prefers games to lessons, Semion Andreich insists. He's only human after all!

Mama listens silently and nods. She puts on her coat, hat, and mittens. She pulls on her boots. But then she remembers that she forgot to drink some water. She pulls off her boots.

"Do you want some water?"

"No!" Semion Andreich shakes his head.

While Mama gulps from a big glass, Semion Andreich nags her about the negative impact of speech therapy lessons on a certain small, but nevertheless quite chubby-cheeked boy.

"Come on, I'll tell you about the knights." Mama puts down her water.

"What knights?" Semion Andreich's interest is instantly sparked.

"The knights from the playset Grandma and Grandpa gave you for your birthday. Do you want to hear about them?"

"Yeah!"

"Did you look closely at their armor?" Mama pulls on her boots.

"I did," Semion Andreich hesitantly confirms.

"Good work."

So, all the way to Alevtina Petrovna's house—eight metro stops, one long park, and two underpasses—Mama tells him about the Knights Templar. How powerful they were, the long crusades they set off on, and how they founded new kingdoms in the Near East. Semion Andreich is all eyes and ears. He prompts her with questions.

"Did they eat on the horses with forks and knives?" he asks, for example.

"On what horses?" Mama stops short.

"On their war horses."

Mama looks at Semion Andreich in surprise. Semion Andreich looks at Mama in surprise. Well, what was so strange about his question? If knights went on crusades for many years, then where did they eat, drink, and sleep? On the backs of their trusty horses, of course!

"So they ate with their hands, then?" Semion Andreich frets.

"And here we are," Mama cheerfully proclaims and punches in the code for Alevtina Petrovna's entry door.

Alevtina Petrovna always smells like sweets. Sometimes like cinnamon buns, and sometimes like cookie rings sprinkled with nuts. Semion Andreich inhales deeply and is clearly suffering. Now they will torment him yet again with various exercises. As if Semion Andreich doesn't understand that it's really just another lesson . . .

Alevtina Petrovna spreads out letter blocks on the table, chairs, television, windowsill, and even the broad leaf of the rubber plant.

"Now, let's play detective," she announces, pleased with her inventiveness. "Now bring me, Semion Andreich dear, the block with the syllable *SHO*."

Since Semion Andreich is a Knight Templar in training, he accepts the conditions of Alevtina Petrovna's game without argument. One should not upset a noble lady who smells like cinnamon buns and cookies with rejection!

Semion Andreich sighs, falls into formation with the crusaders, and sets out on a quest for this wretched block with the syllable *SHO*.

The block is on the coffee table, behind a pile of thick books. Semion Andreich makes a dismal face and trots over to Alevtina Petrovna with a resigned expression. Why a resigned expression? Because he knows what's coming next. He wasn't born yesterday.

"Well done, clever boy!" Alevtina Petrovna's face breaks into a broad smile and she takes the block from him. "And now, let's repeat what's written on it. *Sho*! *Shhhh-o*!"

Semion Andreich has had an awkward relationship with the sound *sh* for a long time. Maybe it's because *sh* is playing tricks on him or maybe the time is never right, but either way, every time Semion Andreich tries to conquer the sound, it rudely turns over on his tongue and transforms into *s*. Semion Andreich can't tolerate such an insult, so he responds to *sh* in kind—he stubbornly ignores it.

Alevtina Petrovna doesn't understand these nuances and torments Semion Andreich with various exercises.

"Raise the tip of your tongue to your palate," she instructs him.

If Semion Andreich knew where his palate was, he would have somehow sorted it out himself. But Semion Andreich forgets where this palate is every single time, and he helplessly turns to Mama. Mama makes her eyes round, opens her mouth wide, and points to the location of the palate.

"*Sh-sh-sh-sh-sho*-oulder!" Alevtina Petrovna sings.

"Uh-oulder!" Semion Andreich stubbornly hoots.

Mama is ready for the earth to swallow her whole.

"Semion!" She throws her hands up. If Mama calls him just Semion, it means she's ver-r-r-r-ry angry.

"I don't want to say that word!" Semion Andreich sniffs.

"How will you learn to make the sound if you don't even try to pronounce it?" Mama asks.

Alevtina Petrovna drums her fingertips on her knee. Suddenly, her face lights up. She goes into the other room and comes back with a big sugar cookie.

"Let's do it this way," she suggests. "If you'll give the sound a try, I'll give you this sugar cookie. How about that? Repeat after me: *shu*-gar. *Sh-sh-sh-shu*-gar."

Semion Andreich really loves sugar. Really really. In his ranking of favorite things, sugar comes right after Grandpa. Mama is first, then Papa, then Grandma, then Grandpa, then sugar. Then his bicycle.

But even a personal ranking won't make Semion Andreich give up his principles and call sugar "sooger." So Semion Andreich bursts into tears and runs into the hall to put on his coveralls.

"We put in some good work today. Thank you, dear," Alevtina Petrovna says in parting.

"Thanks to your lessons, he's been learning to read and write very quickly," Semion Andreich's mama awkwardly tries to excuse him.

"Why don't you skip tomorrow's lesson? Let the child rest," Alevtina Petrovna decides.

"What am I going to do with you?" Mama sighs as they exit onto the stairway landing.

Semion Andreich guiltily picks at the wall with his finger. He has nothing to say.

After dinner, Mama hands him the sugar cookie.

"Alevtina Petrovna gave you this. Maybe now, though, you can sing the word *sugar*. Just once!"

Semion Andreich stamps his feet and sulks silently.

"Fine, go," Mama says.

That night, she discovers the cookie on Semion Andreich's table. The cookie is sitting on top of his drawing book. A reproachful entry snarls on the page in prickly block letters:

THIS IZ A SWEET KOOKY.

Semion Andreich Goes Skiing

Semion Andreich got it wrong—Mama didn't buy the skis as a birthday surprise for herself. She was planning to go skiing. The very next day, early in the morning, as soon as she turned in the next article for her colorful magazine.

When he found out about Mama's plans, Semion Andreich milled around the apartment all evening with a worried look. He checked the supply of Grandpa's bruise and backache ointment in the medicine cabinet. Grandpa pulled out his back so often that he kept some everywhere. Even in the garage.

In the medicine cabinet, in addition to the ointment, he found an elastic bandage, iodine, and disinfectant. Also, some sort of tablets that were pretty-looking and terrifyingly effective.

"All of this will come in handy," Semion Andreich decided.

Right after New Year's, Mama decided to lose weight. And from that moment on, Semion Andreich didn't have a moment's rest. First, Mama signed up for aerobics. After the first lesson, she lay face up on the floor for three days and was afraid to even blink because all her muscles were sore, literally all of them, even the ones that were "out of the way."

A week later, she signed up for water aerobics. Muscles don't get sore from water aerobics because the lessons take place in the pool, and the water reduces the strain.

Mama doesn't really know how to swim, or, to be exact, she doesn't know how to swim at all. But the instructor said she could wear a special belt during the lesson that would keep her from sinking.

"You'll be held up like a buoy," he assured her.

Mama bought a beautiful swimsuit, dark blue with light blue swirls, and she went to her water aerobics. A pale instructor brought her home. In his own car. While Semion Andreich revived him with tea, he explained how Mama had put in a solid effort that day. According to him, she had started to sink even before getting in the pool, and she swallowed so much water at the lesson that the swimmers ended up sitting on the bottom.

"I've never seen anything like it!" the instructor shook his head and loudly slurped his soothing mint tea from a big painted mug.

Mama listened, her eyes downcast, and didn't say a word. She just washed down the pool water with a tablet. To prevent indigestion.

After that, she decided to go on morning runs. But she considered the time of year, how it was winter outside, and she bought herself skis. To coordinate with the season.

"Skiing tones the body and brightens the complexion," Mama encouraged herself the next morning, fastening her coat. Semion Andreich, dressed in his full getup—skis in one hand, poles in the other, a real fur *ushanka* hat on his head, special boots on his feet—called up the elevator. Unlike Mama, he could ski pretty well because he learned from Papa.

"How does it tone the body?" he asked.

"Well," Mama dragged her skis onto the stairway landing, "the body becomes thin and in shape. Hold the elevator, I'll be right there."

Across the street from Semion Andreich's house stretched a big park. It was covered with snow up to its ears. On weekends, there were a lot of skiers there. They skied in formation around a special track, and they even organized competitions. Now Mama had decided to join them.

Semion Andreich spouted instructions the entire way. Mama listened with half an ear, snagged her skis on people walking by, and then got completely tangled up in the lattice fence. She barely managed to free herself. While Semion Andreich showed her the right way to fasten the binding, she gathered her courage for a battle march around the park.

"I'll manage, I'll surely manage!" she whispered.

"Hello!" a familiar, mocking voice rang out behind her back. "You've decided to ski for a bit?"

"Papa!" Semion Andreich squealed, and with a running start, threw his arms around Papa's neck. "You're back!"

"I'm back, Semion Andreich. I got back last night." Papa picked up Semion Andreich and whirled him in the air. "Hello, son, I've missed you very much."

"Hello, Andrei," Mama said.

"Hello, Katya," Papa went to kiss her on the cheek, but she turned away.

Semion Andreich has a separated family. This sort of thing sometimes happens to children. The parents get divorced, and the papa goes away to live with another woman. Or the mama goes away to live with another man. Semion Andreich is understanding of his parents' divorce because they were honest with him about everything.

"We'll live separately, but we'll love you just as much as always. And even twice as much!" they promised.

"All right, then," Semion Andreich agreed.

Papa went away for a month to scuba dive in the tropics. But now he was finally back! Sun-tanned, white-toothed, and handsome!

"Papa, I got a bicycle for my birthday. And a playset," Semion Andreich boasted.

"And I brought you a real scuba mask. And flippers."

"Hooray!"

"Katya, can I take him for today? We'll go to the movies and get ice cream."

"He has his lesson at three o'clock," Mama reminded them.

"We'll go to Alevtina Petrovna's, too."

"Fine."

Papa has a new wife. She's half Scottish, and her name is Charlotta. Charlotta the Scot. It's like some sort of taunt! Semion Andreich doesn't call her by her name. Only "you." Aunt Charlotta understands. She teaches Semion Andreich English words. Thanks to her, Semion Andreich knows how to politely say "khellow," "tenk you," and "gud bai."

Mama calls Papa's new wife a toothpick behind her back. Charlotta probably also calls Mama something similar. It's obvious that they're not overly fond of each other.

"Well, I'm off now," he nodded towards his wife.

"Helloo there," Aunt Charlotta's hand waved from afar.

"Khellow!" Semion Andreich shouted.

Mama smiled at Charlotta in a way that made Charlotta blink fearfully.

"We're off, Semion Andreich! Time to ski."

"I'm coming, just let me put my skis on."

While Semion Andreich fastened the binding of his skis, Mama watched Papa and Charlotta. They went out onto the ski track, flowed into the general group, and sped along.

"Just what I need," Mama sniffed and tried to budge from her place. Semion Andreich wanted to show her the right way to do it, but it was already too late—Mama flew face-first into the snow, her skis crossed beautifully in flight and her poles flung wide.

"Help me get over there, and somehow I'll make it on my own," she hooted from the snowbank.

Semion Andreich singlehandedly pushed Mama to the ski track.

"This is the beginner's lane," a girl in a dark blue coat pointed, "practice here for now."

"I'll go in front, and you go behind. I'll teach you," Semion Andreich offered.

"All right," Mama agreed.

For a while, she more or less kept up behind Semion Andreich. Then she fell onto her side. As luck would have it, that very minute Papa and Charlotta went past.

"Starting is half the battle," Papa shouted.

"No one asked you," Mama snapped. Getting up, she stepped on one ski with the other and fell all over again. This time, for variety, she fell onto her other side. Semion Andreich felt every bit of her pain.

"How about a break?" he suggested.

"All right."

Mama got up somehow, leaned on her poles, and took in the park with a general's gaze. In the distance, Charlotta skied with measured strides, unfaltering in her pace.

"Hmph," Mama bristled and pushed off with her poles, "if we're going to ski, let's ski!"

During their second lap, Papa and Charlotta caught her wallowing in the snow. Semion Andreich was just putting her fallen-off cap back on her head, and she was unhooking one ski from the other.

The next time Papa and Charlotta skied past, Mama lay in the pose of a starfish, her arms and legs beautifully splayed.

"Katya, maybe you've had enough?" Papa was concerned.

"That's not for you to decide," Mama responded and cast a long, unblinking stare at Papa and Charlotta. Charlotta skied as if she had a powerful engine running somewhere inside her. Mama sighed.

"Okay, Semion Andreich, I'll sit quietly on the bench, and you can ski a bit."

"Mmhm," Semion Andreich readily agreed.

While he skied to and fro within Mama's view, she drew some sort of symbols in the snow with her ski pole. Her pom-pom hat periodically slid down over her eyes, and she adjusted it with a frost-covered mitten.

During his next lap, Papa snatched up Semion Andreich and set him on his shoulders.

"A-a-a-a-ah," Semion Andreich began to squeal.

"Be kairfool, Andrei hooney," Charlotta shouted from behind.

"Everything's fine, darling!"

Semion Andreich began to squirm, trying to position himself so his skis weren't in Papa's way.

"Everything's all right, don't fidget," Papa responded. "So tell me, how are you progressing with the sound *sh*?"

"Nothing yet," Semion Andreich mumbled.

"But you know what I like most of all about what you said?"

"What?"

"The word 'yet.' It means you won't give up. And someday, you'll pronounce the sound *sh* without a doubt. If not today, then tomorrow. Got it?"

"Got it."

They went the rest of the way in silence. Semion Andreich wrapped his arms around Papa's neck and closed his eyes in happiness. There he was, his beloved Papa, dearest and wonderful, the one-and-only in the whole world!

"Katya, I'll come by for him at 12," the one-and-only Papa informed Mama, unloading Semion Andreich onto her lap.

"Okay."

Semion Andreich buried his face in Mama's coat. She smiled and kissed him on the cheek.

"Let's go, you can help me rub Grandpa's ointment on my shoulder. It looks like I pulled it after all!"

That evening, Papa brought Semion Andreich home.

"I hope there won't be any more of these slips of the tongue, bud," he said as they parted.

"What are you talking about?" Mama was alarmed.

"I accidentally called her Aunt Toothpick," Semion Andreich frowned.

Mama's face turned beet red.

"Andrei, the boy didn't mean it. He was repeating what I said."

"Katya, really!"

"That'll be the end, I promise. I won't do it anymore!" Mama assured him.

"I promise too!" Semion Andreich hugged his father. "Please don't be mad at us."

"I won't."

That night, when Mama checked on her son as usual—to tuck him in—Semion Andreich was sleeping with his scuba mask pulled over his face. His flippers playfully stuck out from under the blanket.

Mama sputtered with laughter, darted out of the room, returned with a camera, and took his picture. Then she carefully removed the mask and flippers. On her way out, she glimpsed the drawing book out of the corner of her eye.

Semion Andreich had carefully written the following entry in block letters: ITS OK TO CALL ANT SHARLOTA NISE. BUT NOT A TOOTHPIK.

MASHA RUPASOVA (b. 1975) was born and raised in Moscow. She graduated from Moscow State Pedagogical University, after which she worked as a teacher, magazine editor, and freelance journalist. Becoming a mother of an adopted child inspired her to write children's poetry. She published her poems first on LiveJournal, where the children's poet Marina Boroditskaya read and complimented them. Rupasova's poem "I Am News" brought her immediate Internet fame. Between 2015 and 2020, Rupasova published ten books of poetry for small children, among them *All to the Garden* (2016), *The Tale of the Sausage King* (2018), *Grandma Winter Writes* (2019), and *Grandpa, Here You Are* (2019). She often writes about grandmothers and grandfathers, and about loss and grieving. Some of her collections have been issued as audiobooks. Rupasova also writes children's nonfiction, including the works *Kremlin, from Tower to Tower* (2019), *The History of Moscow* (2021), and *Merry Idioms* (2021). She co-authored the book *The Origin of Humans* (2020) with the anthropologist Stanislav Drobyshevsky, which covers a range of topics from human evolution to creating a YouTube channel. Residing in Vancouver, Canada, Rupasova works to develop inclusive education and anti-bullying programs. The selected poems in this volume are from Rupasova's first collection, *Grandmas Falling from the Sky* (2015).

In the Old Days

Translated by Alexandra Berlina

In the old days, say the wise,
grandmas fell out of the skies—
what a flurry, all was blurry,
what a glorious surprise!
All the grandmas travelled light—
just a star to light the night,
just a star and sweets for children,
and their aprons were all white.
Off they went, not knowing where,
searching for an easy chair;
some got stuck atop a fence . . .
People came to their defence,
wouldn't let them climb and roam,
helped them down and brought them home,
and they settled very well.
Since those times—yes, since they fell
from the blue and sunny skies—
grandmas have been baking pies,
rocking babies very gently,
singing moonlight lullabies.

I Am News

Translated by Alexandra Berlina

Where is Mommy? Far away!
She's been facebooking all day,
busy looking up online
if the planet's doing fine.
There she sits, her back all curled,
checks what happens in the world.
Mom? Hello? You've got to hear:
I am happening
          right here!

Jam

Translated by Alexandra Berlina

If your grandma's making jam,
every little thing's okay:
    everybody's mood,
        your scooter,
            mellow sunshine,
                gentle rain.
Bubbling quietly, the jam
speaks of sweetness and of joy,
    of the crunchy
        crust of bread,
            dipped and licked
                and dipped again.

Great-grandma

Translated by Alexandra Berlina

Great-
grand-
ma,
you are so **old**—
old enough
for "old"
in bold.
You're as wrinkled as a nut.
But
you never hunted dinos,
never slept inside a cave—
was it out of fear or shyness?
Oh, if only you'd been brave!

You are almost eighty-five,
and you've wasted all your life!

ANASTASIA ORLOVA (b. 1981) is the youngest writer represented in this anthology. Born in the Volgograd district and educated in the Tuva Republic and the Republic of Khakassia, she now lives in Yaroslavl. Her first poem was published in the children's magazine *Streetcar* when she was nine years old. Since her first book, *Little Apples, Little Heels* (2012), she has published another twenty books of poetry and prose for small children about everything under the sun: dogs, caterpillars, penguins, cars, seasons, and clouds. Among her books are *River, River, Where Is Your Home?* (2014), *We Are in the Boat* (2015), *Sleepy Book* (2018), and *Do Not Wake the Rhinoceros: ABCs* (2020). Orlova also wrote a guidebook about her city, *Yaroslavl: Stories for Children* (2019). She has received several literary awards, including the Rosman New Children's Book Prize (2011–2012), the 2013 Marshak Prize, and the 2014 and 2020 Chukovsky Prize. Additionally, she received the Russian Federation Presidential Award for Children's Literature (2017). In 2019, Orlova opened her own publishing company Anastasia Orlova's Book House, which specializes in poetry, fiction, and nonfiction for small children. *This Is Truck, and This Is Trailer* (2015) echoes Osip Mandelstam's *Two Trams*. The picture book is illustrated by **Olga Demidova** (b. 1987) and has six sequels, including *Truck and Trailer's Business Trip* (2017) and *Truck, Trailer, and the Christmas Tree* (2017).

Anastasia Orlova, *This Is Truck, and This Is Trailer*, illus. Olga Demidova (Moscow: Rosman, 2017). Courtesy of Rosman Publishing House.

This Is Truck, and This Is Trailer

Translated by Jane Bugaeva

Truck has four wheels and Trailer has four wheels.
Truck has a cargo bed and Trailer has a cargo bed.
Truck holds cargo and Trailer holds cargo.
Truck has a steering wheel but Trailer does not!
Truck has an engine but Trailer does not!
Truck has headlights but Trailer does not!
Trailer has one license plate and Truck has two.
Truck is filled with bricks and Trailer is filled with gravel.
Trailer is working hard but Truck is working even harder.
Wherever Truck goes, Trailer follows.
Truck drives along the road pulling Trailer behind him.
All of a sudden . . .
a pothole!
Truck hits the pothole, "Thump!"
And Trailer hits the pothole, "Thump!"
They keep driving.
Until . . .

a pothole and another pothole!
Truck hits the first pothole, "Thump!" And the second, "Thump!"
Trailer, too, "Thump! Thump!"
They keep driving.
Until . . .
a pothole, a bigger pothole, and an even bigger pothole!
Truck swerves, avoiding the potholes.
But Trailer, "Thump! Thump! Thump!"
Truck drives along the road with Trailer behind him, riding smooth and easy.
They keep driving.
Until . . .
a boom gate! Stop! Construction site!
"What are you hauling?"
"Bricks and gravel."
"Drive on though!"
Truck unloads the bricks, "Thud! Thud! Thud!"
Trailer unloads the gravel, "Crunchy crunch crunch!"
Truck drives away with Trailer behind him.
Truck is empty and Trailer is empty.
Truck feels light as can be, with Trailer bouncing along behind him.
Wherever Truck goes, Trailer follows.
They're happy together.
Truck drives along the road with Trailer behind him, riding smooth and easy.
They keep driving.
Until . . .
a hill.
Time to go up the hill.
Truck braces himself and starts climbing. But Trailer does not want to go up the hill—he would rather roll down it.
Truck pulls Trailer up, up, up.
Trailer drags Truck down, down, down.
Truck huffs and puffs, Truck is annoyed, but Truck keeps going.
Phew! They made it up the hill.
But now . . .
time to go down the hill.
Trailer is excited, "Now I'll get to roll down!"
But Truck drives down slowly, carefully.
Trailer pushes Truck, "Faster! Faster!"
Trailer shoves Truck, "Quicker! Quicker!"

Trailer laughs, bouncing up and down, "Go, go, go!"

Truck barely holds himself back—he does not want to get angry, does not want to go too fast.

Phew! They made it down the hill!

They keep driving.

Until . . .

another hill.

Truck braces himself, revs his engine.

Truck climbs up, up, up.

And up, and up, and up.

And up some more.

And Trailer . . .

Where is Trailer? He's gone! He got unhitched!

He's rolling down the hill! Bump! Bonk! Thud! Thump! Faster! Faster! Faster!

Truck turns around and rushes to help! But it is too late, Trailer flies off the road—he has no steering wheel. And breaks a wheel.

Truck tows out Trailer and hitches him up tighty-tight.

They barely make it up the hill. They barely make it down the hill. Trailer wobbling the whole way.

They drive to a service station. Trailer has to be left there, to get his wheel fixed.

But Truck has work.

Truck goes to pick up watermelons.

Trailer is sad and bored. Trailer is lonely. He can't go left or right or forwards or backwards—he does not have an engine. There is nobody to pull him around. His wheel has long been fixed. But Truck is still not back. There is only a stray dog—who hides under Trailer to escape the hot sun.

Meanwhile, Truck goes to a farm and is loaded up with watermelons. Now he is taking them to the store. Until . . .

a right turn.

Truck turns right. The watermelons in the truck bed roll left.

He keeps driving.

Until . . .

a left turn.

Truck turns left. The watermelons in the truck bed roll right.

He keeps driving.

Until . . .

a traffic light. Red light. Stop!

Truck stops. The watermelons in the truck bed roll forward.

Yay! Green light!

Truck speeds off, the watermelons in the truck bed roll backwards—but one watermelon roll, roll, rolls out and lands in the road, "Crack!"

Truck keeps driving.

Until . . .

a gate! Stop! Grocery store.

"What are you hauling?"

"Watermelons."

"Drive on through!"

Truck unloads the watermelons, "Thunk, thunk, thunk!"

Truck drives away. He's empty and light.

He keeps driving.

Until . . .

chickens.

"Beep, beep!" says Truck.

"Cluck, cluck!" say the chickens and scatter.

He keeps driving.

Until . . .

geese.

"Beep, beep!" says Truck.

"Honk, honk!" say the geese and waddle off.

He keeps driving.

Until . . .

cows.

"Beep, beep!" says Truck.

The cows are silent.

"Beep, beep!" says Truck.

The cows just chew, swinging their tails.

"Beep, beep! Beep, beep! Beep, beep!" says Truck.

The cows don't move!

Cows in the road. Truck in the road.

One minute passes.

Two minutes pass.

Three minutes.

Four.

Five.

Six.

Seven.

Eight.
Nine.
Ten minutes!
Truck is silent.
"Moo," say the cows and go home.
Now Truck can go. He keeps driving.
He is worried, "I hope Trailer isn't lonely! I hope his wheel doesn't hurt!"
Then it starts to rain.
"Drip, drop" goes the rain.
"Swish, swash," go the windshield wipers.
"Pitter, patter," goes the rain.
"Swash, swish," go the windshield wipers.
Truck is racing, he is in a hurry.
Until . . .
a pothole!
Truck hits the pothole, "Thump!"
He keeps driving.
Until . . .
a puddle!
Truck drives through the puddle sending up a spray of water, "Splash!"
He keeps driving.
Until . . .
another pothole, with a puddle inside.
Truck goes, "Thump! Splash!"
But he does not stop. He keeps going.
Oh no! It's getting dark!
Then . . .
another puddle. And lots of mud.
"Splash . . . vroo . . . vroo . . ." Truck is stuck!
"Vrrr . . . Vrrr . . . Vrrr!" No luck.
"Vrrrrrr . . . Vrrrrrr!" Truck is stalled!

Back at the station, Trailer is losing hope. "He's not coming! Truck is not coming to get me! Maybe he got in an accident? Maybe he has abandoned me? He does not need me. It is easier for him without me . . . I only get in his way . . ."

Trailer starts crying.
"Drip drop," go his tears.
"Drip drop," goes the rain.
Drip drop on Dog's nose.

The night is very, very dark. There is nothing around. Even Trailer thinks he does not exist. But wait—what is that light in the distance?

It is Truck!

Hurray!

"Woof, woof!"

Truck is back! He is tired and dirty, but his headlights shine bright.

Trailer hitches onto Truck tighty-tight and together they slowly drive off.

"Beep, beep," says Truck to Dog. "Come with us!"

Trailer trembles and shakes along the dirt path—he is scared he will get unhitched.

A minute ago there was nothing, but now Trailer is surprised to see a road!

Truck's headlights lead the way, on and on, farther and farther, all the way to their garage.

Inside the garage it is warm and cozy.

And Dog is nearby.

Translators' Biographies

ALEXANDRA BERLINA was born in Moscow. She studied in London and completed her PhD in Essen with her dissertation "Brodsky Translating Brodsky: Poetry in Self-Translation." She currently lives in Düsseldorf and works as a translator and interpreter in German, Russian, and English. She has translated works by Artur Givargizov, Sergei Kozlov, Masha Rupasova, O. Henry, Neil Gaiman, and Daniel Kehlmann. Berlina is the editor and translator of the award-winning anthology *Viktor Shklovsky: A Reader* (Bloomsbury, 2016). Her translations of Mikhail Bulgakov's *The Master and Margarita* and *Heart of a Dog* into German were published in 2020 and 2023 (Anaconda).

ILYA BERNSTEIN is a poet and translator. His first collection of poetry is titled *Attention and Man* (Ugly Duckling Presse, 2003). His poetry, prose, and translations have appeared in *Ars Interpres, Circumference, Fulcrum, 6×6, Persephone, Moon City Review,* and *Res.* He is the editor of *Osip Mandelstam: New Translations* (UDP, 2006). His recent publications include a book of poetry, *Distances and Sounds* (Ars Interpres, 2019), a collection of the poems by Osip Mandelstam in English translation (M-Graphics, 2019), and a book of his own work translated into Danish, *Både og* (Det Poetiske Bureaus Forlag, 2020).

JANE BUGAEVA emigrated to the United States from Russia at the age of six. Forever a child at heart, she translates Russian children's literature. Her translations include Anna Starobinets's *Catlantis* (Pushkin Press; NYRB, 2016) and the four-book series *Beastly Crimes* (Dover Publications, 2018–19), as well as Ludmilla Petrushevskaya's *The New Adventures of Helen: Magical Tales* (Deep Vellum, 2021), and the illustrated nonfiction book *The Trans-Siberian Railway* by A. Litvina and A. Desnitskaya (Thames & Hudson, 2021). She lives in North Carolina.

OLGA BUKHINA is a translator, writer, children's books specialist, and independent scholar based in New York City. She has translated over fifty books from English into Russian, primarily children's books. She writes about children's literature for various journals, collections, and online publications in Russian and English. Her books *The Ugly Duckling, Harry Potter, and Others: A Guide to Children's Books about Orphans* (KompasGid, 2016) and *Life and Death: The Most Important Issues of Children's Literature* (KompasGid, 2024) were published in Moscow. She coauthored (with Andrea Lanoux and Kelly Herold) *Growing Out of Communism: Russian Literature for Children and Teens, 1991–2017* (Brill-Schöningh, 2022).

CARA EHLENFELDT is a writer and director with a Bachelor's degree in linguistics from Swarthmore College and a Master's degree in sound arts and industries from Northwestern University. Their work in linguistics and translation focuses on wordplay and child language development in Russian children's literature.

KATYA (KATHERINE) FARBER grew up as a first-generation American in a family of Russian immigrants. Russian was her first language, and she grew up bilingual, able to speak and read in both Russian and English. This sparked a lifelong love of reading, allowing Katya to understand the nuances of both languages and translate between the two. She also speaks French and Spanish. Katya graduated from Fordham University in 2021. She is currently a PhD student at Stony Brook University in the integrative neuroscience program.

SIBELAN FORRESTER is Susan W. Lippincott Professor of Modern and Classical Languages and Russian at Swarthmore College, where she teaches language, literature, and the theory and practice of translation. Most of her scholarly writing (some fifty articles) concerns poetry. She has translated fiction, folktales, poetry, and scholarly prose from Croatian, Serbian, and Russian, including Vladimir Propp's *The Russian Folktale* (Wayne State UP, 2012) and folktales in *Baba Yaga: The Wild Witch of the East in Russian Fairy Tales* (UP of Mississippi, 2013). She is the editor or co-editor of six books, including (with Martha Kelly) *Russian Silver Age Poetry: Texts and Contexts* (Academic Studies Press, 2015).

MICHAEL HENRY HEIM (1943–2012) was a professor of Slavic languages and literatures at the University of California at Los Angeles. Heim taught a workshop in literary translation at UCLA's Department of Comparative Literature, and he was a prolific translator from Croatian, Czech, Dutch, French, German, Hungarian, Italian, Romanian, Russian, and Serbian. Heim translated works by Anton Chekhov, Kornei Chukovsky, Vasily Aksenov, Sasha Sokolov, Milan Kundera, Thomas Mann, Günter Grass, and Dubravka Ugrešić. Eduard Uspensky's *Uncle Fedya, His Dog, and His Cat* is Heim's only translation of a text for children. After Heim's death, he was identified as the anonymous donor behind the PEN Translation Fund.

KELLY HEROLD is a professor of Russian at Grinnell College, where she teaches Russian, the Russian novel and short story, Nabokov, Tolstoy, and a course on American young adult fiction. Continuing her dissertation work on Russian memoir literature, she has published on Nabokov's autobiographies and eighteenth-century Russian memoirs written in French. She has published commentaries on the collected works of Aleksandr Sumarokov and articles on the portrayal of Baba Yaga in American picture books and teen fiction in Russia. She coauthored (with Andrea Lanoux and Olga Bukhina) *Growing Out of Communism: Russian Literature for Children and Teens, 1991–2017* (Brill-Schöningh, 2022).

ANNA KRUSHELNITSKAYA was born on Sakhalin Island in the Soviet Far East. She grew up in the Siberian city of Chita. Anna taught English and translation theory at the university level in Russia before moving to the US in 2004. Her articles on language pedagogy have appeared in *Modern English Teacher, ESL Magazine,* and scholarly journals in Russia. She enjoys writing, literary translation, and blogging on Soviet topics. Krushelnitskaya's translations appear in various online journals and in collections of Soviet World War II poetry and contemporary Russian free verse. She published *Cold War Casual* (Front Edge Publishing, 2019), a collection of transcribed oral testimonies, in both Russian and English. Her poetry collection, *A False Nanny* (Front Edge Publishing), came out in 2021. In 2025, together with Dmitri Manin, she published *Firefly in a Box: An Anthology of Soviet Kid Lit* (University of Missouri Press).

ANDREA LANOUX is Elizabeth S. Kruidenier '48 Professor of Slavic Studies at Connecticut College, where she has been teaching Russian language and culture since 1999. She co-edited *Gender and National Identity in Twentieth-Century Russian Culture* with Helena Goscilo (Northern Illinois UP, 2006), and she has published articles on Russian children's literature, Polish women's magazines, the poets Adam Mickiewicz and Anna Świrszczyńska, and literary canon formation. Along with Kelly Herold and Olga Bukhina, she is coauthor of the book *Growing Out of Communism: Russian Literature for Children and Teens, 1991–2017* (Brill-Schöningh, 2022).

DMITRI MANIN is a physicist, programmer, and poetry translator. His translations from English and French into Russian have appeared in several book collections. His latest work is a complete translation of Ted Hughes's *Crow* (Jaromír Hladík Press, 2020) and Allen Ginsberg's *Howl, Kaddish and Other Poems* (Podpisnye Izdaniya, 2021). Manin's Russian-to-English translations have been published in the journals *Cardinal Points, Delos, The Café Review,* and *Metamorphoses,* among others, and in Maria Stepanova's *The Voice Over*

(Columbia UP, 2021). In 2017, his translation of Stepanova's poem "Saturday and Sunday burn like stars" won the Compass Award competition. *Columns*, translations of Nikolai Zabolotsky's poems, was published by Arc Publications in 2023. In 2025, together with Anna Krushelnitskaya, Manin published *Firefly in a Box: An Anthology of Soviet Kid Lit* (University of Missouri Press).

AINSLEY MORSE teaches at the University of California San Diego and translates Russian and former Yugoslav literatures. Published translations include Vsevolod Nekrasov's *I Live I See* (Ugly Duckling Presse, 2013, with Bela Shayevich); *Kholin 66: Diaries and Poems* (UDP, 2017, with Bela Shayevich); Andrei Egunov-Nikolev's *Beyond Tula: A Soviet Pastoral* (Academic Studies Press, 2019), and, with Philip Redko, a collection of Yuri Tynianov's theoretical essays: *Permanent Evolution* (Academic Studies Press, 2019). Recent publications include *F-Letter: New Russian Feminist Poetry* (isolarii, 2020, edited with Galina Rymbu and Eugene Ostashevsky) and the Introduction to Lida Yusupova's *The Scar We Know* (Cicada Press, 2021). She also translated the Yugoslav surrealist-Marxist epic poem for children, written by Aleksandar Vučo, "Fine Feats of the Five Cockerels Gang" (with Aleksandar Bošković, Brill, 2022), and the Odesan poet Maria Galina's *Communiqués* (with Anna Halberstadt, Cicada Press, 2024).

JAMIE OLSON is a professor of English at Saint Martin's University, a small Benedictine institution in Lacey, Washington. His essays and translations from Russian have recently appeared in *America Magazine, Translation Review,* and *100 Poems about Moscow: An Anthology*. In 2017, he received an NEA Translation Fellowship to support his work translating the poetry of Timur Kibirov. Jamie lives with his wife and daughter in Olympia.

EUGENE OSTASHEVSKY was born in Leningrad, grew up in New York, and lives mainly in Berlin. His book of poetry *The Pirate Who Does Not Know the Value of Pi,* published by NYRB Poets (2017), discusses migration, translation, and second-language writing as practiced by pirates and parrots. His recent publications include *The Fire Horse: Children's Poems by Mayakovsky, Mandelstam, and Kharms* (NYRB Children, 2017) and *The Feeling Sonnets* (NYRB Poets, 2022). His translations and editions include *OBERIU: An Anthology of Russian Absurdism* (Northwestern UP, 2006), Alexander Vvedensky's *An Invitation for Me to Think* (NYRB Poets, 2013; winner of the 2014 National Translation Award from the American Literary Translators Association), and *F-Letter: New Russian Feminist Poetry,* co-edited with Galina Rymbu and Ainsley Morse (isolarii, 2020).

LYDIA RAZRAN STONE began learning Russian as a teenager when her father told her that, since she loved literature, she needed to read Tolstoy in the original. She earned a Master's degree in Russian literature and worked for ten years for NASA abstracting Russian space biology and medicine journals for English-speaking NASA researchers. Subsequently she began translating Russian poetry into the original meter, working as a poetry translator for Russian Life books. She has published five dual-language books of translated Russian poetry, and for twenty-five years she was the editor of *SlavFile,* the journal of the American Translators Association.

MATVEI YANKELEVICH is a poet, translator, and editor based in New York. His translations from Russian include works by Elena Guro, Daniil Kharms, Osip Mandelstam, Vladimir Mayakovsky, and Alexander Vvedensky. He is a translator of *Today I Wrote Nothing: The Selected Writings of Daniil Kharms* (The Overlook Press, 2007). He has been awarded fellowships for translation from the National Endowment for the Arts and the National Endowment for the Humanities, and he was a co-recipient (with Eugene Ostashevsky) of the 2014 National Translation Award for *An Invitation for Me to Think* by Alexander Vvedensky (NYRB Poets, 2013). He founded and edited the Eastern European Poets Series for Ugly Duckling Presse. He is an editor at World Poetry, a non-profit publisher of poetry in translation. He teaches translation at Columbia University's School of the Arts.

KATHERINE E. YOUNG is the author of *Woman Drinking Absinthe* (Alan Squire Publishing, 2021) and *Day of the Border Guards* (University of Arkansas Press, 2014; Miller Williams Arkansas Poetry Prize finalist), and the editor of *Written in Arlington.* Young has translated many recent titles, including Anna Starobinets's *Look at Him* (Slavica Pub, 2020), Akram Aylishli's *Stone Dreams* (Academic Studies Press, 2022) and *Farewell, Aylis* (Academic Studies Press, 2019), and Inna Kabysh's *Blue Birds and Red Horses* (Toad Press, 2018) and *Two Poems* (Artist's Proof Editions, 2014). Her translations of contemporary Russian-language poetry have won international awards; she was named a 2017 National Endowment for the Arts translation fellow. From 2016 to 2018, she served as the inaugural Poet Laureate for Arlington, Virginia.

Alphabetical List of Authors and Titles in Russian

Абгарян, Наринэ, *Семен Андреич. Рукопись в каракулях* [отрывок]
Барто, Агния, “В школу”
“Дом переехал”
“Перед сном”
“Уехали”
Бианки, Виталий, “Как муравьишко домой спешил”
“Сова”
Булычев, Кир, “Бронтя”
Введенский, Александр, “Колыбельная”
“Кто?”
Гиваргизов, Артур, *Генералы* [отрывок]
Записки выдающегося двоечника [отрывок]
Голявкин, Виктор, “На балконе”
Григорьев, Олег, “Велосипед меня понес”
“С длинным батоном под мышкой”
“Таракан на столе”
Драгунский, Виктор, “Главные реки Америки”
Есеновский, Михаил, *Главный шпионский вопрос* [отрывок]
Житков, Борис, “Про обезьянку” [отрывок]
Заболоцкий, Николай, “Сказка о кривом человечке”
Заходер, Борис, “Диета термита”
“Ежик”
“Кискино горе”
“Никто”
“Повара”
Зощенко, Михаил, “Елка”
“Как Ленин перехитрил жандармов”
Каверин, Вениамин, “Много хороших людей и один завистник” [отрывок]
Козлов, Сергей, “Ежик в тумане”
“Как ежик с медвежонком протирали звезды”
Мандельштам, Осип, “Два трамвая”

Additional Resources

Aromsham, Marina. *The Real Boat*. Illus. Viktoria Semykina. London: Templar, 2019.

Belyaev, Roman. *How Does a Lighthouse Work?* Trans. Masha Kulikova, Sam Hutchinson, and Jenny Jacoby. London: b small publishing, 2018.

Belyaev, Roman. *How Do Bridges Work?* Trans. Ruth Ahmedzai Kemp. London: b small publishing, 2020.

Brodsky, Joseph. *Discovery*. Illus. Vladimir Radunsky. New York: Farrar Straus Giroux, 1999.

Chukovsky, Kornei. *Mishmash*. Illus. Francesca Yarbusova. Trans. Luba Golburt. San Francisco: Rovakada Publishing, 2011.

Chukovsky, Kornei. *Telephone*. Illus. Vladimir Radunsky. Trans. Jamey Gambrell. New York: North-South Books, 1996.

Denisevich, Kasya. *Neighbors*. San Francisco: Chronicle Books, 2020.

The Fire Horse: Children's Poems by Vladimir Mayakovsky, Osip Mandelstam and Daniil Kharms. Trans. Eugene Ostashevsky. New York: NYR Children's Collection, 2017.

Kharms, Daniil. *The Charms of Harms*. Trans. Svetlana Dubovitskaya. London: Matteo Publishing, 2011.

Kozlov, Sergei, and Yuri Norstein. *Hedgehog in the Fog*. Illus. Francesca Yarbusova. Trans. Luba Golburt. San Francisco: Rovakada Publishing, 2010.

Lissitzky, El. *About Two Squares: A Suprematist Tale of Two Squares in Six Constructions*. Trans. Odile Belkeddar. London: Tate Publishing, 2015.

Marshak, Samuil. *Baggage*. Illus. Vladimir Lebedev. Trans. Jamie Gambrell. London: Tate Publishing, 2013.

Marshak, Samuil. *The Circus and Other Stories*. Illus. Vladimir Lebedev. Trans. Stephen Capus. London: Tate Publishing, 2013.

Marshak, Samuil. *Hail to Mail*. Illus. Vladimir Radunsky. Trans. Richard Pevear. New York: Henry Holt & Co, 1990.

Marshak, Samuil. *The Pup Grew Up*. Illus. Vladimir Radunsky. Trans. Richard Pevear. New York: Henry Holt & Co, 1989.

Sedoff, Serge. *Heracles' 12 Great Labours*. Illus. Tatiana Kormer. Trans. Melanie Moore. London: St. Jim's Press, 2015.

Starobinets, Anna. *Catlantis*. Trans. Jane Bugaeva. New York: NYR Children's Collection, 2016.

Starobinets, Anna. *In the Wolf's Lair: A Beastly Crimes Book*. Trans. Jane Bugaeva. Mineola, NY: Dover Publications, 2018.

Starobinets, Anna. *A Predator's Rights: A Beastly Crimes Book* (#2). Trans. Jane Bugaeva. Mineola, NY: Dover Publications, 2019.

Starobinets, Anna. *Claws of Rage: A Beastly Crimes Book* (#3). Trans. Jane Bugaeva. Mineola, NY: Dover Publications, 2019.

Starobinets, Anna. *The Plucker: A Beastly Crimes Book* (#4). Trans. Jane Bugaeva. Mineola, NY: Dover Publications, 2019.

Uspensky, Eduard. *Uncle Fedya, His Dog, and His Cat.* Trans. Michael Henry Heim. New York: Alfred A. Knopf, 1993.

Uspensky, Eduard. *Crocodile Gene and His Friends.* Trans. Nina Ignatowicz. New York: Alfred A. Knopf, 1994.

Uspensky, Eduard. *The Little Warranty People.* Trans. Nina Ignatowicz. New York: Alfred A. Knopf, 1994

Bibliography

Balina, Marina, and Eugeny Dobrenko, eds. *Petrified Utopia: Happiness Soviet Style*. London: Anthem Press, 2009.

Balina, Marina, Helena Goscilo, and Mark Lipovetsky, eds. *Politicizing Magic: An Anthology of Russian and Soviet Fairy Tales*. Evanston, IL: Northwestern University Press, 2005.

Balina, Marina, and Serguei Alex. Oushakine, eds. *The Pedagogy of Images*. Toronto: University of Toronto Press, 2021.

Balina, Marina, and Larissa Rudova, eds. *Russian Children's Literature and Culture*. New York: Routledge, 2008.

Balina, Marina, and Larissa Rudova, eds. "Special Forum Issue: Russian Children's Literature: Changing Paradigms." Special issue, *Slavic and East European Journal* 49, no. 2 (Summer 2005).

Balina, Marina, Larissa Rudova, and Anastasia Kostetskaya, eds. *Historical, Literary, and Cultural Transformations of Russian Childhood*. New York: Routledge, 2022.

Bukhina, Olga, ed. "Russian Children's and Young Adult Literature." Special issue, *Russian Studies in Literature* 52, no. 2 (2016).

Bukhina, Olga, ed. "Women Writers and Girl Characters in Russian Children's Reading." Special issue, *Russian Studies in Literature* 55, nos. 3-4 (2019).

Goodwin, Elena. *Translating England into Russian: The Politics of Children's Literature in the Soviet Union and Modern Russia*. London: Bloomsbury Academic, 2019.

Hellman, Ben. *Fairy Tales and True Stories: The History of Russian Literature for Children and Young People (1574–2010)*. Leiden: Brill, 2013.

Kelly, Catriona. *Children's World: Growing Up in Russia, 1890–1991*. New Haven, CT: Yale University Press, 2007.

Krushelnitskaya, Anna, and Dmitri Manin, eds. *Firefly in a Box: An Anthology of Soviet Kid Lit*. Columbia: University of Missouri Press, 2025.

Lanoux, Andrea, Kelly Herold, and Olga Bukhina. *Growing Out of Communism: Russian Literature for Children and Teens, 1991–2017*. Paderborn: Brill-Schöningh, 2022.

Morse, Ainsley. *Word Play: Experimental Poetry and Soviet Children's Literature*. Evanston, IL: Northwestern University Press, 2021.

Ostashevsky, Eugene, ed. *OBERIU: An Anthology of Russian Absurdism*. Evanston, IL: Northwestern University Press, 2006.

Oushakine, Serguei Alex, ed. "Transmediating Children's Books: An Archaeology of Discarded Futures: A Special Cluster of Essays." Special issue, *Russian Review* 80, no. 3 (July 2021).

Panaou, Petros, and Janelle Mathis, eds. "A Special Issue on Russian Children's Literature." Special issue, *Bookbird* 58, no. 2 (2020).

Reynolds, Kimberley, Jane Rosen, and Michael Rosen, eds. *Reading and Rebellion. An Anthology of Radical Writing for Children, 1900–1960*. Oxford: Oxford University Press, 2018.

Rothenstein, Julian, and Olga Budashevskaya. eds. *Inside the Rainbow: Russian Children's Literature 1920–1935: Beautiful Books, Terrible Times*. London: Redstone Press, 2013.

Shteiner, Evgeny. *Stories for Little Comrades: Revolutionary Artists and the Making of Early Soviet Children's Books*. Seattle: University of Washington Press, 1999.

Swift, Megan. *Picturing the Page: Illustrated Children's Literature and Reading under Lenin and Stalin*. Toronto: University of Toronto Press, 2020.

Voronina, Olga, ed. *A Companion to Soviet Children's Literature and Film*. Leiden: Brill, 2019.

Weld, Sara Pankenier. *An Ecology of the Avant-Garde Picturebook*. Amsterdam: John Benjamins Publishing Company, 2018.

Weld, Sara Pankenier. *Voiceless Vanguard: The Infantilist Aesthetic of the Russian Avant-Garde*. Evanston, IL: Northwestern University Press, 2014.

White, Elizabeth. *A Modern History of Russian Childhood: From the Late Imperial Period to the Collapse of the Soviet Union*. London: Bloomsbury, 2020.

List of Copyrights

Russian Texts Copyrights

Narine Abgaryan, *Semion Andreich: The Scribble Chronicles* [excerpts] © 2025 by Banke, Goumen, and Smirnova Literary Agency.

Agnia Barto, "The House That Moved," "They Left," "Off to School," "Bedtime" © 2025 by A. Barto, heirs.

Vitaly Bianki, "The Owl," "The Little Ant Who Hurried Home" © 2025 by V. Bianki, heir.

Kir Bulychev, "Bronty" © 2025 by K. Bulychev, heir.

Kornei Chukovsky, "Roach the Terrible" © 2025 by K. Chukovsky, heir.

Viktor Dragunsky, "The Main Rivers" © 2025 by V. Dragunsky, heir.

Mikhail Esenovsky, *The Essential Spy Question* [excerpts] © 2025 by M. Esenovsky.

Artur Givargizov, *Notes of a Distinguished F Student* [excerpts], *Generals* [select poems] © 2025 by A. Givargizov.

Viktor Golyavkin, "On the Balcony" © 2025 by Rosman Publishing House.

Oleg Grigoriev, "Something Crawled onto the Table," "My Bicycle Carried Me Away," "A Boy Bought Some Bread at the Store" © 2025 by O. Grigoriev, heirs.

Veniamin Kaverin, "Many Good People and One Envious One" [excerpts] © 2025 by V. Kaverin, heirs.

Sergei Kozlov, "Hedgehog in the Fog," "Hedgehog, Bearcub, and the Dust on the Stars" © 2025 by S. Kozlov, heir.

Samuil Marshak, "Baggage" © 2025 by S. Marshak, heir.

Sergei Mikhalkov, "Uncle Styopa" © 2025 by S. Mikhalkov, heir.

Anastasia Orlova, *This Is Truck, and This Is Trailer* © 2025 by Rosman Publishing House.

Grigory Oster, *Horrible Advice: A Book for Disobedient Children and Their Caregivers* [select poems] © 2025 by G. Oster.

Ludmilla Petrushevskaya, *Piglet Peter Drives a Car, Piglet Peter at the Store* © 2025 by Rosman Publishing House.

Irina Pivovarova, "We Searched the World Both Far and Wide," "When…," "Teeny Tiny Pony," "The Violin" © 2025 by I. Pivovarova, heir.

Alexander Raskin, "How Papa Chose His Profession" © 2025 by A. Raskin, heir.

Masha Rupasova, "In the Old Days," "I Am News," "Jam," "Great-grandmother" © 2025 by M. Rupasova.

Dina Sabitova, *Circus in a Treasure Box* [excerpts] © 2025 by Samokat Publishing House.

Genrikh Sapgir, "Wonder Woods," "The Princess and the Ogre" © 2025 by G. Sapgir, heir.

Sergei Sedov, *Tales about a Boy Named Alex* [excerpts] © 2025 by S. Sedov.

Andrei Usachev, *Smart Dog Sonya* [excerpts] © 2025 by A. Usachev.

Eduard Uspensky, *Uncle Fedya, His Dog, and His Cat* [excerpts] © 2025 by Alfred A. Knopf Publishing House.

Mikhail Yasnov, "Counting-Rhyme," "Kitty-cat and Ratty-rat," "Us and Birds," "Autumn Grandpa," "A Little Tree with Wings" © 2025 by M. Yasnov, heir.

Nikolai Zabolotsky, "The Tale of the One-Eyed Little Man" © 2025 by N. Zabolotsky, heirs.

Boris Zakhoder, "Kitty's Sorrow," "Hedgehog," "Cooks," "No One," "The Termite's Diet" © 2025 by B. Zakhoder, heir.

Mikhail Zoshchenko, "The New Year's Tree," "How Lenin Tricked the Police" © 2025 by M. Zoshchenko, heirs.

Translations Copyrights

Sergei Kozlov, "Hedgehog in the Fog," "Hedgehog, Bearcub, and the Dust on the Stars"; Artur Givargizov, *Notes of a Distinguished F Student* [excerpts], *Generals* [select poems]; Masha Rupasova, "In the Old Days," "I Am News," "Jam," "Great-grandmother" © 2025 by Alexandra Berlina.

Daniil Kharms, "Mr. Golden Samovar," "Once There Was a Little Man," "Why Don't We Write a Story?"; Boris Zhitkov, "Yashka" [excerpt] © 2025 by Ilya Bernstein.

Aleksey Tolstoy, *The Golden Key, or the Adventures of Buratino* [excerpts]; Oleg Grigoriev, "Something Crawled onto the Table," "My Bicycle Carried Me Away," "A Boy Bought Some Bread at the Store"; Grigory Oster, *Horrible Advice: A Book for Disobedient Children and Their Caregivers* [select poems]; Andrei Usachev, *Smart Dog Sonya* [excerpts], Ludmilla Petrushevskaya, *Piglet Peter Drives a Car, Piglet Peter at the Store*; Anastasia Orlova, *This Is Truck, and This Is Trailer* © 2025 by Jane Bugaeva.

Mikhail Yasnov, "Counting-Rhyme"; Boris Zakhoder, "The Termite's Diet" © 2025 by Olga Bukhina.

Narine Abgaryan, *Semion Andreich: The Scribble Chronicles* [excerpts] © 2025 by Cara Ehlenfeldt.

Viktor Dragunsky, "The Main Rivers" © 2025 by Katya Farber.

Kir Bulychev, "Bronty" © 2025 by Sibelan Forrester.

Eduard Uspensky, *Uncle Fedya, His Dog, and His Cat* [excerpts] © 2025 by Michael Henry Heim. Reproduced with permission from Alfred A. Knopf Publishing House.

Mikhail Esenovsky, *The Essential Spy Question* [excerpts] © 2025 by Kelly Herold.

Kornei Chukovsky, "Roach the Terrible"; Mikhail Zoshchenko, "The New Year's Tree," "How Lenin Tricked the Police"; Agnia Barto, "The House That Moved," "They Left," "Off to School," "Bedtime"; Emma Moshkovskaya, "I Was Very Mean to My Mommy" © 2025 by Anna Krushelnitskaya.

Vitaly Bianki, "The Owl," "The Little Ant Who Hurried Home"; Dina Sabitova, *Circus in a Treasure Box* [excerpts] © 2025 by Andrea Lanoux.

Emma Moshkovskaya, "Clever Old Ladies," *Tales of Little Goat and Little Donkey* [excerpt]; Genrikh Sapgir, "Wonder Woods," "The Princess and the Ogre" © 2025 by Dmitri Manin.

Vladimir Mayakovsky, "What Is Good and What Is Bad"; Daniil Kharms, "Ivan van Littleaxe"; Nikolai Zabolotsky, "The Tale of the One-Eyed Little Man"; Boris Zakhoder, "Kitty's Sorrow,"

"Hedgehog," "Cooks," "No One"; Mikhail Yasnov, "Counting-Rhyme," "Kitty-cat and Ratty-rat," "Us and Birds," "Autumn Grandpa," "A Little Tree with Wings" © 2025 by Ainsley Morse.

Sergei Mikhalkov, "Uncle Styopa"; Sergei Sedov, *Tales about a Boy Named Alex* [excerpts] © 2025 by Jamie Olson.

Osip Mandelstam, "Two Trams" © 2025 by Eugene Ostashevsky. Reproduced with permission from The New York Review Children's Collection.

Daniil Kharms, "A Man Left His House" © 2025 by Eugene Ostashevsky and Matvei Yankelevich. Reproduced with permission from Northwestern University Press.

Samuil Marshak, "Baggage"; Alexander Vvedensky "Lullaby" © 2025 by Eugene Ostashevsky.

Irina Pivovarova, "We Searched the World Both Far and Wide," "When…," "Teeny Tiny Pony," "The Violin" © 2025 by Lydia Razran Stone.

Alexander Vvedensky, "Who?" © 2025 by Matvei Yankelevich.

Veniamin Kaverin, "Many Good People and One Envious One" [excerpts]; Alexander Raskin, "How Papa Chose His Profession"; Viktor Golyavkin, "On the Balcony" © 2025 by Katherine E. Young.

www.ingramcontent.com/pod-product-compliance
Lightning Source LLC
Chambersburg PA
CBHW060620310726
48982CB00003B/625

* 9 7 9 8 8 8 7 1 9 8 5 9 0 *